A SENSE OF HISTORY

The Making of the United Kingdom

Crowns, Parliaments and Peoples, 1500–1750

JAMES MASON

ANGELA LEONARD
Assessment Consultant

LONGMAN

Acknowledgements

We are grateful to the following for permission to reproduce copyright photographs:

Ashmolean Museum, Oxford, page 81 *above*; Record Office, Bedford County Council, page 60 *below*; Bibliothèque et Universitaire, Geneva, page 27; The Bodleian, University of Oxford, pages 25 D.I.I. Th. Seld., 105 *below*; By permission of the Birmingham Museum and Art Gallery, page 113 *above left*; Private Collection/Bridgeman Art Library, page 33, Tichborne Park, Hampshire/Bridgeman, page 52, Hatfield House, Herts/Bridgeman page 54, National Maritime Museum/ Bridgeman, page 68, Private Collection/Bridgeman, page 84 *above*, Museum of London/Bridgeman, page 92 *above*, Coram Foundation/Bridgeman, page 113 *below right*, British Library, London/Bridgeman, page 115, City of Bristol Museum and Art Gallery/Bridgeman, page 127; By permission of the British Library, pages 5 *Bm Roy. Ms. IIE..xi*, 9 *Add. 15760 68v 69*, 10 *Bm Roy. Ms. 20E. ix.ff.29 b-30*, 13 *below left Bm Ms. 1852-5-19-2*, 55 *below*, 78, 84 *below*, 95 *left and right*; Reproduced by courtesy of the Trustees of the British Museum, page 105 *above*; The Governors of Christ's Hospital/photo by Derek Witty, page 104 *left*; College of Arms, page 8 *The Great Tournament Roll of Westminster*; English Heritage, page 24; Faculty of Advocates/photo by Edinburgh Photo Library, page 117; The Fotomas Index, pages 19, 20, 23, 35, 62, 63, 66, 70, 77, 79, 80, 97 *below left*, 103 *right*, 106; Glasgow Museums, page 94; From *Chequers, The Country Home of Britain's Prime Ministers*, by Plantagenet Somerset Fry. Reproduced with the permission of the Controller of HMSO, page 71; Michael Holford, pages 103 *left*, 114, 126; A.F Kersting, page 116; By permission of the Masters and Fellows, Magdalene College, Cambridge, page 92 *below*; 'Sir Thomas Aston at the Deathbed of his Wife', by John Souch, © Manchester City Art Galleries, page 57; Mansell Collection, pages 30 *above and below*, 81 *below*, 85, 88, 90, 91, 107; Trustees of the National Library of Scotland, page 118; Reproduced by courtesy of the Trustees, The National Gallery, London, pages 34, 97 *above right*; The Trustees of the National Museums of Scotland 1992, page 47 *above*; National Portrait Gallery, London, pages 4 *right*, 37, 53, 73, 110, 113 *above right*, 113 *below left*; National Trust of Scotland, page 47 *below*; RCHME/Palace of Westminster Picture Collection, page 121; Royal Collection, St. James's Palace, © Her Majesty the Queen, pages 12, 13 *above*, 67, 109, 123; Sheldonian Theatre/University of Oxford, page 104 *right*; Society of Antiquaries of London, page 4 *left*; L.G. Stopford Sackville, page 125; The Tate Gallery, London, page 56; University of Oxford, © Museum of the History of Science, page 100 *above*, 102 *above*; Wellcome Institute Library, London, page 100 *below*, 102 *below*; Welsh Folk Museum, Cardiff, page 55 *above*; Andy Williams, page 60 *above*; Simon Wingfield Digby, Sherbourne Castle, © Private Collection, page 17; Woodmansterne/Westminster Abbey, page 7; The Worshipful Company of Barbers, page 13 *below right*.

We have been unable to trace the copyright from the photographer of the painting on page 104 *left*, and would be grateful for any information that would enable us to do so.

Cover Photograph: Tichborne Park, Hampshire/Bridgeman Art Library (Detail).

Picture Research by Sandie Huskinson-Rolfe (PHOTOSEEKERS)

Longman Group UK Limited
*Longman House, Burnt Mill, Harlow, Essex, CM20 2JE, England
and Associated Companies throughout the World*

© Longman Group UK Limited 1992

First published 1992
Second impression 1992
ISBN 0 582 20737 1

*Typeset in Monotype Lasercomp 12/14pt Photina
Printed in Hong Kong*
NPC/02

*The publisher's policy is to use paper manufactured
from sustainable forests*

*Designed by Michael Harris
Illustrated by Tong Richardson, The Wooden Ark Studio*

Contents

1   Tudors and Stuarts   4

2   Crown and Government   7

3   Crown, Church and People   22

4   The Kingdoms of the British Isles   37

5   Four Sorts of People   51

6   Civil War   66

7   Republic and Restoration   80

8   Science and Superstition   99

9   The 'Glorious Revolution'   109

10 The United Kingdom and Ireland   117

11 Luxuries and Manufactures   126

1
Tudors and Stuarts

In 1485 Henry Tudor, Earl of Richmond, defeated and killed King Richard III at the battle of Bosworth Field. This turned out to be the last battle of the civil wars, known as the Wars of the Roses, in which barons from the rival families of York and Lancaster fought for the throne. The battle of Bosworth Field decided the matter in favour of the Lancastrians and Henry Tudor became King Henry VII (source 1).

Before the battle, Henry took an oath saying that if he became king he would marry Elizabeth of York (source 2), daughter of the Yorkist King Edward IV, and so unite the two rival families. In 1486 he kept his promise.

To show that he stood for a united and peaceful country, Henry VII combined the Lancastrian red rose with the Yorkist white rose to make a double rose (source 3) which became the emblem of

SOURCE 1

King Henry VII of England. This is one of several pictures painted in 1515–21 on wooden panels all cut from the same tree.

SOURCE 2

Elizabeth of York. This portrait was probably painted to make a pair with source 1.

the Tudors. He also used the red dragon (source 3), the emblem of Welsh royal princes. Henry VII's grandfather, Owain ap Meredith ap Tewdwr, was a Welsh landowner and Henry himself was born and brought up in Wales. All the Tudors were proud of their Welsh ancestry.

SOURCE 3

Tudor emblems. A picture at the front of a book of music made in 1516. Find:
- the garden with a wall round it, surrounded by sea. This stands for England
- the lion of England guarding the gate
- the red roses of Lancaster and white roses of York
- the double rose with the crown on it
- the red dragon of the Welsh royal princes.

Henry had been a rebel himself and his great fear was that others would rebel against him. His ambitions were to make the country safe, peaceful and wealthy, and to ensure that his own son rather than a rival would follow him as king. He managed to achieve both.

Henry and Elizabeth founded the Tudor line of rulers (source 4). Their son became King Henry VIII and then three of his children, Edward, Mary and Elizabeth, each became **monarch** in turn.

Henry VII and Elizabeth of York also linked the Tudor royal family to the Stuart royal family of Scotland (source 4). In 1503 they married their eldest daughter, Margaret, to the son of King James IV of Scotland.

So, when Queen Elizabeth I died in 1603, leaving no children, and the Tudor line ended, the English invited James VI of Scotland to be their next king because of his relationship to Henry VII and Elizabeth of York. He became James I of England, the first of the Stuart line of kings and queens of England.

i **Monarch** *A king or queen.*

SOURCE 4

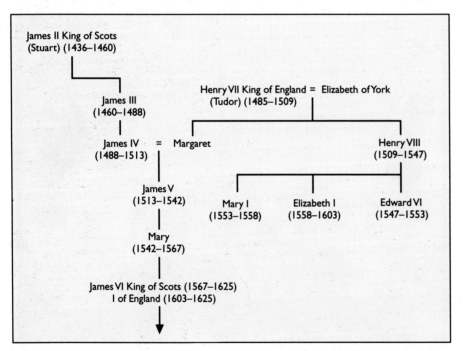

The links between the English Tudor royal family and the Scottish Stuart royal family.

SOURCE 5

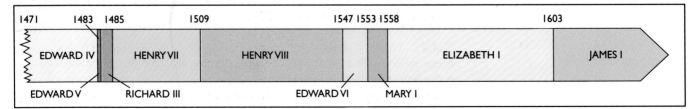

Kings and queens of England, 1471–1603.

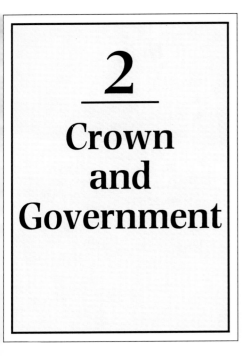

2
Crown and Government

What was expected of a king?

Henry VII's funeral

SOURCE 1

Henry VII's tomb in Westminster Abbey. The King is shown lying beside Elizabeth of York who died in 1503. Henry VII wanted a grand tomb. Henry VIII ordered it to be specially made by the Italian sculptor Pietro Torrigiano, who began the work in 1512 and finished it in 1518.

On 10 May 1509 a procession of lords and bishops made its way slowly through the streets of London towards Westminster Abbey. They were following a carriage pulled by five horses draped in black. On the carriage lay the dead body of Henry VII.

A funeral is a time for remembering what was good about someone and the things they had achieved. One of the bishops, John Fisher, made a speech at Henry's funeral:

SOURCE 2

His wisdom in governing the country was exceptional, his intelligence always quick and ready . . . his speech gracious in many languages, his looks good and amiable [friendly] . . .

He made alliances with all Christian princes, his mighty power was dreaded everywhere . . . His people were obedient to him . . . his land many a day in peace . . . his good fortune in battle marvellous . . . [his] treasure and riches incomparable, his buildings most goodly.

John Fisher's speech at Henry VII's funeral, 1509

activity

Work in pairs.
I Look at source 2.
a What can you learn from it about what people expected of a king?
b Fisher was bound to say good things about Henry VII. Is his speech still useful in telling us about the things people expected from a king?

Henry VIII

Henry VII's seventeen-year-old son became the new king, Henry VIII. He was the first king to succeed to the throne peacefully since 1422.

He became king at a time of change in Europe, when artists and scholars were looking at the world in new ways and asking new questions about it. Rulers were still expected to be strong fighters (source 3) and they were also expected to be well-educated and have an interest in music, paintings and fine buildings.

SOURCE 3

Henry VIII breaking his lance on an opponent while jousting in a tournament in front of his queen, Catherine of Aragon, in 1512. He took part in tournaments until he was knocked unconscious for two hours in 1536. His father, Henry VII, never jousted himself, but he used to give money and prizes for tournaments and sometimes acted as a judge.

activity

2 Look at sources 3 and 4 and the information in the text.
a What qualities do they tell you people admired in a king?
b How were these different from the qualities people admired in a Medieval king?

Henry VIII fitted people's idea of this new kind of king very well. London was full of ambassadors from other countries whose job was to keep their own rulers informed of what was going on. This is how the Venetian ambassador described Henry in 1519:

SOURCE 4

His majesty . . . is extremely handsome . . . a good musician, composes well, is a most capital [excellent] horseman, a fine jouster, speaks French, Latin and Spanish, is very religious . . .

Letter from the Venetian ambassador, 1519

Europe and the world

Another change which was taking place when Henry VIII became king was that people's knowledge about the lands and seas of the world was growing very quickly. In the fifteenth century explorers started to sail to places that had never been visited by Europeans before (source 5).

SOURCE 5

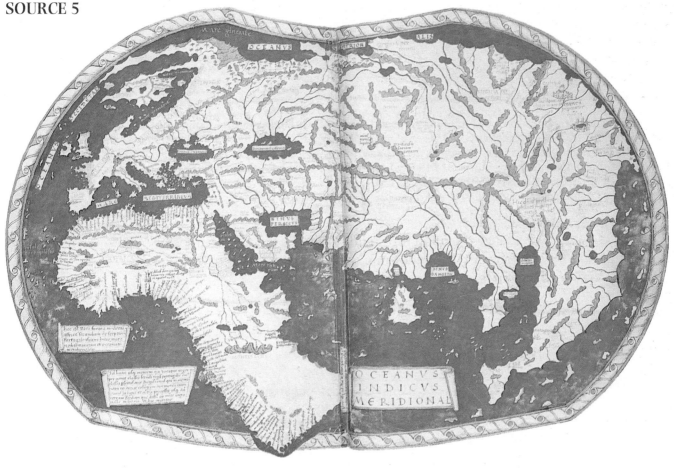

Henricus Martellus's map of the world, made in about 1489, just before Henry VIII was born. Portuguese sailors had been exploring the west coast of Africa since the early fifteenth century in search of a sea route to India, shown on the right of the map. In 1487 Bartolomeo Dias sailed round the Cape of Good Hope, at the bottom of Africa. You can tell from the map how far he got before turning back for home.

SOURCE 6

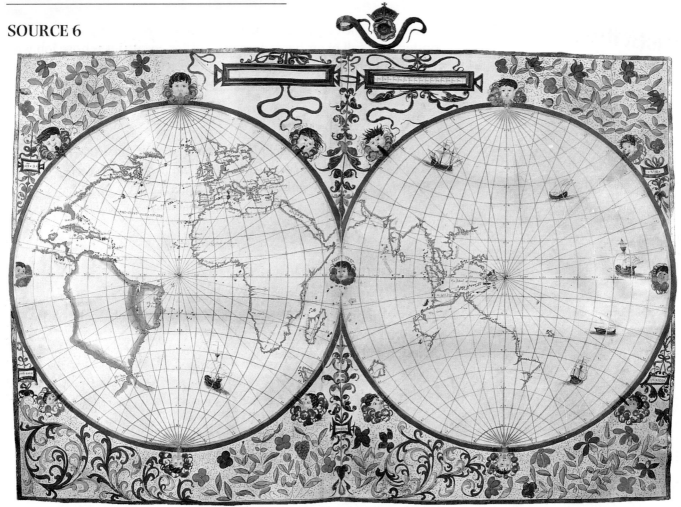

A map of the world drawn in 1542 by John Rotz, map and chart maker to Henry VIII. By this time the Portuguese had reached India (1498) and Christopher Columbus had made his four voyages (1492–1504) from Spain to the Caribbean, believing he had managed to find a route across the Atlantic to Japan. John Cabot made the same mistake when he reached the coast of Canada in a voyage from Bristol (1497) which was supported by Henry VII. Others realised they had reached a new continent altogether, the 'New World'. Between 1519 and 1522 a Spanish expedition, led by Ferdinand Magellan who died before it was completed, was the first to sail round the world.

The voyages went on throughout Henry's lifetime. He took a great interest in them and employed map makers to provide him with up-to-date maps (source 6).

activity

1 Use sources 5 and 6 to make a list of information that Europeans found out about the world between about 1489 and 1542.
2 Compare sources 5 and 6 with a modern map of the world.
a Which parts of the old maps were the most accurate?
b Why do you think those parts were the most accurate?
c Which lands and seas did John Rotz (source 6) still not know about in 1542?

The British Isles

In 1509 Henry VIII became King of England and Wales, and Lord of Ireland. The other kingdom in the British Isles (source 7) was Scotland which James IV had ruled since 1488.

SOURCE 7

The British Isles in 1500.

Ireland

Gaelic was the main language.
English spoken in towns and area around Dublin, known as the 'Pale'.
Divided into lordships. Some were ruled by descendants of the Norman–English barons who conquered and took over the land in the Middle Ages. Others were ruled by Gaelic lords. The English king claimed 'Lordship of Ireland', but his power was effective only in the Pale and some English lordships beyond it.

[T]he Church

[C]hristianity was the common [r]eligion throughout the British [Isl]es. The Pope in Rome was [th]e overall head of the Church [in] all countries, but kings [us]ually appointed bishops who [als]o helped them to govern. [Th]e Archbishop of Canterbury [ha]d authority over bishops in [En]gland, Wales and the parts [of] Ireland under English [lo]rdship. In Scotland and the [re]st of Ireland, bishops dealt [dir]ectly with the Pope.

Scotland

Gaelic was spoken in the Highlands; a Scottish version of English in the Lowlands.
Ruled by the Stuart family since 1406. Royal power was strong in the Lowlands, less strong in Highlands.
Scotland was allied to France.

Wales

Welsh was the main language.
Divided into two regions. The lands conquered by Edward I in the thirteenth century – now called the Principality – were divided into shires, followed English laws and were ruled by the Crown. The rest was split into Marcher lordships, which, until recently, had been ruled by almost independent barons. Many of these lordships were now in the hands of the Crown, but they still followed Welsh laws and many local lords kept special rights and privileges.

England

English was the common language, though different dialects were spoken in some areas.
Ruled by the Tudor family since 1485.

KEY
- Principality of Wales
- the 'Pale'

SHETLAND

WESTERN ISLES

ORKNEY

0   100km

HIGHLANDS

SCOTLAND

Edinburgh
R. Forth   R. Tweed

LOWLANDS

R. Tees

MAN   York

R. Shannon

Dublin

IRELAND

ENGLAND

WALES

R. Severn

R. Thames

London

N
W   E
S

activity

3a Use the information in source 7 to make a map of the British Isles using colours to show where you think the power of:
- Henry VIII of England
- James IV of Scotland

was (i) strongest, (ii) less strong, (iii) weakest.
b What does your map tell you about the power of monarchs in the early sixteenth century?

Power and pageantry

Henry VII was very careful about spending money and so his son inherited plenty of it. This suited Henry VIII because he thought a monarch should show how powerful and successful he was by spending money on ceremonies and pageantry, as well as on ships and soldiers.

Many pictures and objects have survived from Henry VIII's time. They provide clues about his work as king, what he thought was important and what people expected of him.

SOURCE 8

The embarkation at Dover. A detail from a painting showing Henry VIII setting off to meet the French king. Find:
- the fort. Henry built forts along the south coast of England as a defence against a possible invasion by the French. They were specially designed to withstand gunfire while allowing their own guns to fire in all directions
- the guns. They were a new and expensive type of gun made of bronze
- the King standing on the lower deck in the middle of the ship above the fort. This is his flagship, the 'Henry Grace a Dieu', popularly known as the 'Great Harry'. It was his newest and biggest ship. Henry built forty-six large ships in his reign. In fact, he had to use a smaller ship that day as Dover harbour was too silted up with mud to allow big ships to enter it. Why do you think the artist showed 'Great Harry' anyway?

activity

Work in pairs.
1 Look at source 8.
a (i) In what way is it not completely accurate?
(ii) Make a list of the sorts of things it can tell you about Henry VIII and his times, even though it is not completely accurate.
b How does it show that Henry VIII thought the defence of his kingdom was important?
2 What does source 10 tell you about Henry VIII's attitude to a foreign ambassadors, b artists?
3 How do sources 8 and 9 suggest that Henry VIII thought it was important to impress foreign kings?
4 Does source 11 show that Henry VIII was a generous king? Explain your reasons.
5 Look at sources 8–11.
a How do they show that Henry VIII spent a lot of money?
b Can they tell you whether or not the money was well spent?

i **Hans Holbein** *was a German painter who first visited England between 1526 and 1528. He returned in 1532 and the King paid him a regular salary as Court painter.*

i **Company of Barber Surgeons** *Barbers were hairdressers who, although untrained, had been allowed to do minor operations such as pulling teeth. Surgeons were trained doctors who had been given permission to carry out operations. The Company was formed in 1540 to control the work of both groups and to make sure that, in future, barbers did no surgery at all.*

SOURCE 9

A painting of the meeting in 1520 between Henry VIII and Francis I of France outside the French town of Guisnes. The event is known as 'The Field of the Cloth of Gold' because the Kings met in a tent made of gold cloth. This picture, which was painted about twenty years later, shows several different scenes. Find:
- Henry entering Guisnes in procession (bottom left)
- his temporary palace (bottom right). It had brick foundations, wooden walls and real glass in the windows
- the Kings meeting in the tent of gold cloth (top centre)
- jousting (top right)
- a dragon firework let off by the English (top left).

SOURCE 10

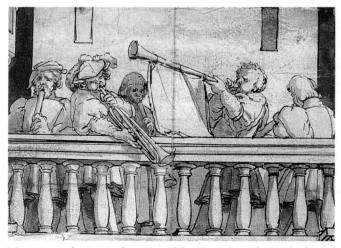

Musicians playing in honour of the French ambassador's visit to Henry VIII at Greenwich Palace in 1527. This sketch is probably by **Hans Holbein**.

SOURCE 11

A gold cup presented by Henry VIII to the **Company of Barber Surgeons**, probably in 1543. As well as giving cups like this on special occasions, Henry gave every member of his Court, including servants, a gold cup or bowl on each New Year's Day. In return they had to give the King a gift according to their wealth.

How did the Crown govern the realm?

The Crown

Henry VIII was a royal person who held the special position, or office, of King. It is useful to be able to talk about the office of King or Queen without meaning a particular king or queen. To do this we use the word 'Crown'. The Crown means the person wearing the crown, the person holding the office of King or Queen.

In the sixteenth century, the Crown was responsible for governing the realm. People expected the Crown to make laws, to keep law and order and give out justice, and to defend the realm against attack.

The system of government

The Crown was the centre of government, but it relied on advice and help from many people, ranging from important lords to ordinary people in their parishes. Source 12 shows you how the system worked.

SOURCE 12

How the Crown governed.

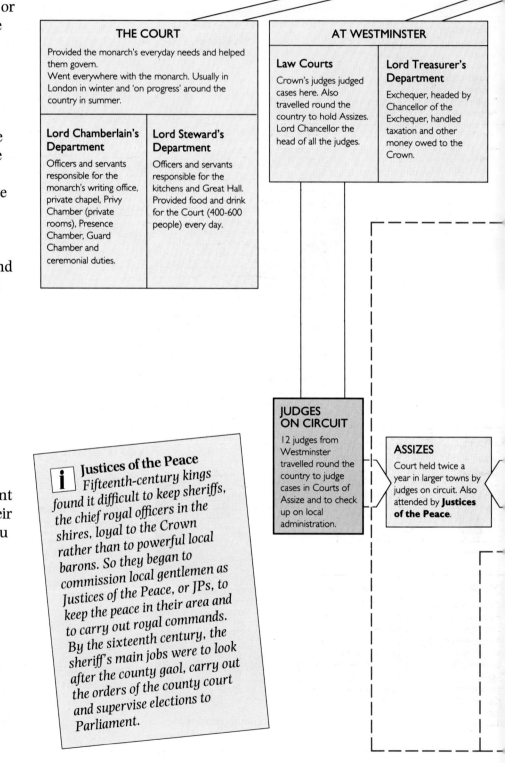

THE COURT

Provided the monarch's everyday needs and helped them govern.
Went everywhere with the monarch. Usually in London in winter and 'on progress' around the country in summer.

Lord Chamberlain's Department

Officers and servants responsible for the monarch's writing office, private chapel, Privy Chamber (private rooms), Presence Chamber, Guard Chamber and ceremonial duties.

Lord Steward's Department

Officers and servants responsible for the kitchens and Great Hall. Provided food and drink for the Court (400-600 people) every day.

AT WESTMINSTER

Law Courts

Crown's judges judged cases here. Also travelled round the country to hold Assizes. Lord Chancellor the head of all the judges.

Lord Treasurer's Department

Exchequer, headed by Chancellor of the Exchequer, handled taxation and other money owed to the Crown.

JUDGES ON CIRCUIT

12 judges from Westminster travelled round the country to judge cases in Courts of Assize and to check up on local administration.

ASSIZES

Court held twice a year in larger towns by judges on circuit. Also attended by **Justices of the Peace**.

ℹ **Justices of the Peace**
Fifteenth-century kings found it difficult to keep sheriffs, the chief royal officers in the shires, loyal to the Crown rather than to powerful local barons. So they began to commission local gentlemen as Justices of the Peace, or JPs, to keep the peace in their area and to carry out royal commands. By the sixteenth century, the sheriff's main jobs were to look after the county gaol, carry out the orders of the county court and supervise elections to Parliament.

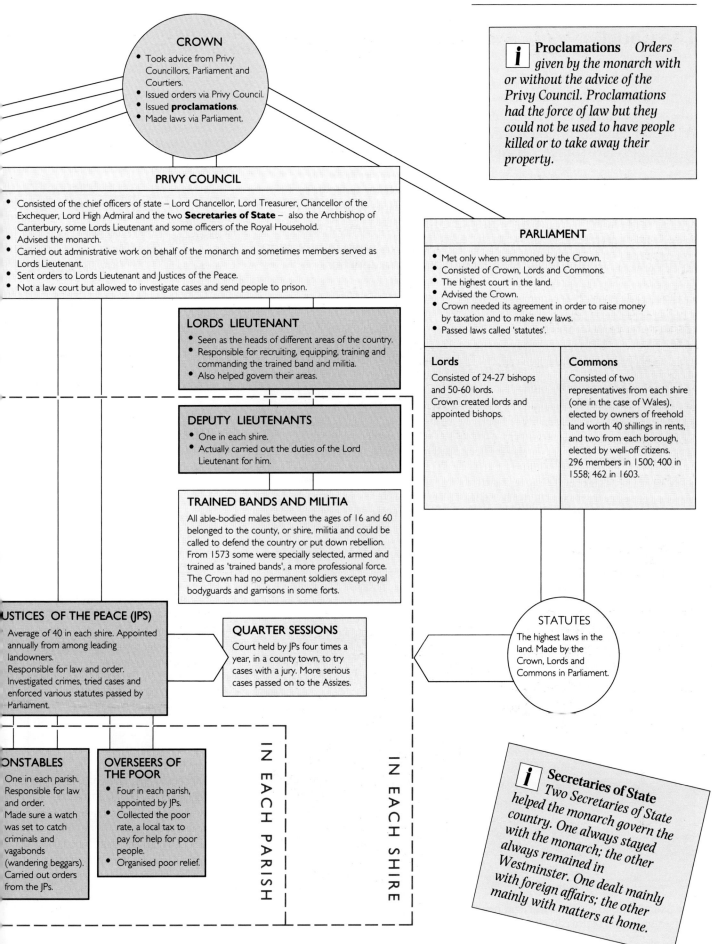

CROWN
- Took advice from Privy Councillors, Parliament and Courtiers.
- Issued orders via Privy Council.
- Issued **proclamations**.
- Made laws via Parliament.

> **i** **Proclamations** *Orders given by the monarch with or without the advice of the Privy Council. Proclamations had the force of law but they could not be used to have people killed or to take away their property.*

PRIVY COUNCIL
- Consisted of the chief officers of state – Lord Chancellor, Lord Treasurer, Chancellor of the Exchequer, Lord High Admiral and the two **Secretaries of State** – also the Archbishop of Canterbury, some Lords Lieutenant and some officers of the Royal Household.
- Advised the monarch.
- Carried out administrative work on behalf of the monarch and sometimes members served as Lords Lieutenant.
- Sent orders to Lords Lieutenant and Justices of the Peace.
- Not a law court but allowed to investigate cases and send people to prison.

PARLIAMENT
- Met only when summoned by the Crown.
- Consisted of Crown, Lords and Commons.
- The highest court in the land.
- Advised the Crown.
- Crown needed its agreement in order to raise money by taxation and to make new laws.
- Passed laws called 'statutes'.

Lords
Consisted of 24-27 bishops and 50-60 lords.
Crown created lords and appointed bishops.

Commons
Consisted of two representatives from each shire (one in the case of Wales), elected by owners of freehold land worth 40 shillings in rents, and two from each borough, elected by well-off citizens. 296 members in 1500; 400 in 1558; 462 in 1603.

LORDS LIEUTENANT
- Seen as the heads of different areas of the country.
- Responsible for recruiting, equipping, training and commanding the trained band and militia.
- Also helped govern their areas.

DEPUTY LIEUTENANTS
- One in each shire.
- Actually carried out the duties of the Lord Lieutenant for him.

TRAINED BANDS AND MILITIA
All able-bodied males between the ages of 16 and 60 belonged to the county, or shire, militia and could be called to defend the country or put down rebellion. From 1573 some were specially selected, armed and trained as 'trained bands', a more professional force. The Crown had no permanent soldiers except royal bodyguards and garrisons in some forts.

JUSTICES OF THE PEACE (JPS)
Average of 40 in each shire. Appointed annually from among leading landowners.
Responsible for law and order.
Investigated crimes, tried cases and enforced various statutes passed by Parliament.

QUARTER SESSIONS
Court held by JPs four times a year, in a county town, to try cases with a jury. More serious cases passed on to the Assizes.

STATUTES
The highest laws in the land. Made by the Crown, Lords and Commons in Parliament.

CONSTABLES
One in each parish.
Responsible for law and order.
Made sure a watch was set to catch criminals and vagabonds (wandering beggars). Carried out orders from the JPs.

OVERSEERS OF THE POOR
- Four in each parish, appointed by JPs.
- Collected the poor rate, a local tax to pay for help for poor people.
- Organised poor relief.

IN EACH PARISH

IN EACH SHIRE

> **i** **Secretaries of State** *Two Secretaries of State helped the monarch govern the country. One always stayed with the monarch; the other always remained in Westminster. One dealt mainly with foreign affairs; the other mainly with matters at home.*

The Court

The monarch spent the winter in various palaces in London and the summer months travelling around the country 'on progress', visiting other royal houses or staying with local landowners (source 13). Wherever the king or queen went, they were always accompanied by the Court (see source 12) and surrounded by their **courtiers** (source 14).

Because courtiers lived close to the monarch they were very important people. They could influence the monarch with their advice and they could ask for jobs and other special favours for themselves or their friends. Anyone from a well-known family, who wanted to get on in the world, hoped to become a courtier.

i **Courtiers**   People whose job was to attend the monarch. These included privy councillors, chief officers of the Lord Chamberlain's and Lord Steward's departments and departments of state, important lords and royal favourites, who were people the king or queen particularly liked and chose to be their close companions. There were also people from well-known families who were given posts such as Lady or Gentleman of the Bed Chamber or Maid of Honour.

SOURCE 13

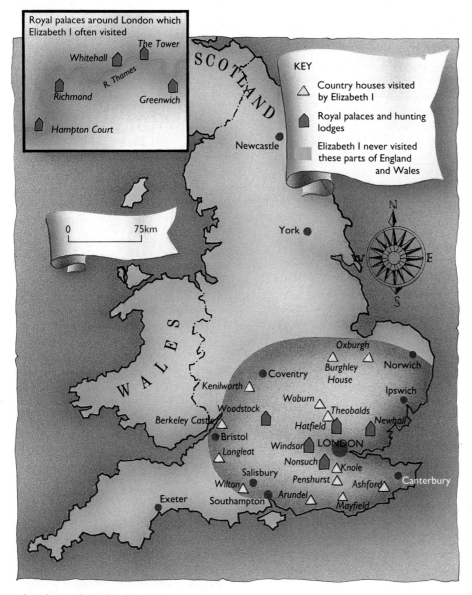

The places that Elizabeth I visited on her progresses. Henry VIII went on progress in the same parts of the country.

activity

1 Look at source 13.
a What parts of the country did Henry VIII and Elizabeth not visit?
b What reasons can you think of for this?
2a Here is the start of a list of the things which happened when the German envoy visited Elizabeth I (source 15):

1 *Gentlemen Pensioners led him to the Presence Chamber;*
2 *He waited in the Presence Chamber.*

(i) Complete the list in chronological order using source 15 and the information in the text.
(ii) How you think the envoy felt at each stage of his reception?
b Do you think the Duke of Wurttemberg was pleased with his envoy's reception? Explain your reasons.

SOURCE 14

Elizabeth I being carried by her courtiers in 1600.

Visitors from other countries were received at Court. Everything was very carefully organised. A German envoy, or messenger, visiting Elizabeth I (Henry VIII's daughter who ruled 1558–1603) described how ten **Gentlemen Pensioners** led him into the Presence Chamber where he waited. Then:

SOURCE 15

The Lord Chamberlain came . . . and led me into the Privy Chamber . . . Both the Privy Chamber and the Presence Chamber were full of Mylords, Grandees, Earls, Lords and of very grand countesses and ladies, who were all without exception beautiful . . . Her Majesty with arms outstretched came half-way up the room to meet me, where I with due reverence [respectfully] kissed her hand. Her Majesty then turned back and seated herself on a chair under a canopy of cloth and gold.

Letter to the Duke of Wurttemberg from his envoy, late fifteenth century

ℹ️ **Gentleman Pensioners** Royal bodyguards, usually young men from well-known families starting off their career at Court.

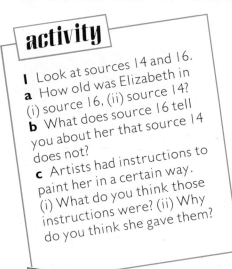

activity

1 Look at sources 14 and 16.
a How old was Elizabeth in (i) source 16, (ii) source 14?
b What does source 16 tell you about her that source 14 does not?
c Artists had instructions to paint her in a certain way. (i) What do you think those instructions were? (ii) Why do you think she gave them?

i **Hoarding**   *Keeping goods in store so as to make them scarce. This made their price go up.*

Another German visitor described the Queen herself in 1598, as she passed in procession through the Presence Chamber on the way to prayers:

SOURCE 16

Next came the Queen, in the sixty-fifth year of her age, very majestic, her face fair but wrinkled, her eyes small yet black and pleasant, her nose a little hooked, her teeth black [from the English habit of too great use of sugar]. She had in her ears two pearls with very rich drops; she wore false hair and that red; upon her head she had a small crown and she had on a necklace of exceeding fine jewels.

Hentzner, 1598

Local government

Justices of the Peace (JPs) more or less ruled the shires on behalf of the Crown. Even though they were unpaid, the Privy Council gave them more and more work to do. For example, in 1544 there were fears that people were **hoarding** grain. Justices were ordered to:

SOURCE 17

Search the houses, barns and yards of . . . persons . . . accustomed . . . to sell corns or grain.

Proclamation concerning corn and grain, 1544

JPs met for the Quarter Sessions (see source 12). At other times they worked alone or in small groups:

SOURCE 18

25 October, 1580
The Lord Cobham and I licensed James Hawkes . . . and George Colt . . . to keep alehouses in their dwelling houses . . .

25 November, 1580
I and my father-in-law took order for the punishment of Joan Pitchford of Seal . . . and Alice Hylles . . . for the bearing of two bastards, and for the punishment of Thomas Byrd . . . and Thomas Pigeon . . . of the same town . . . the reputed fathers . . . Thomas Byrd and Alice were set in a cart at Sevenoaks the next day . . . and Joan scourged [whipped] at the same cart's tail . . . As for Pigeon he was fled long before . . .

23 January, 1581
John Wood of Westminster, waterman, was by us committed to the gaol for robbing Henry Blower of Southwark, wax chandler, on Gad's Hill . . .

From the journal of William Lambarde, Justice of the Peace, 1580–81

activity

2 Look at source 17. Imagine you are one of the JPs who receives this order. Make a list of the things you will have to do in order to carry it out properly.
3 Use sources 17 and 18 to make a list of the different kinds of tasks that JPs had to carry out.
4 Look at source 18.
a Why do you think Thomas Pigeon ran away?
b What might Joan Pitchford think about that?

Parliament

Parliament in the sixteenth century

By 1500 **Parliament** had a definite place in the government of the realm. If the Crown wanted to raise money by taxing people or wanted to make a new law, it had to ask Parliament first and Parliament had to agree.

> **i** **Parliament** The word 'parliament' or 'parlement' came from an old French word 'parlemenz', meaning 'discussion', which came in turn from 'parler', meaning 'to speak'. The word was first used in the thirteenth century to describe the discussions held in the king's Great Councils.

SOURCE 19

Elizabeth I addressing Parliament, from a late seventeenth-century book. The Queen sits in the Parliament House with the Lords. The Commons, led by the Speaker, stand to listen at the bar of the House which they are not allowed to go beyond.

...

Commons Knights from the shires and burgesses from the boroughs. First invited to parliaments in the thirteenth century. Always invited from the end of the fourteenth century. Met separately from the Lords in their own meeting place in the chapter house of Westminster Abbey. Moved to St Stephen's Chapel in Westminster Palace during Edward VI's reign (1547–53).

Lords The barons, bishops and abbots who originally formed the Medieval kings' Great Council. After 1540 there were no abbots to attend because Henry VIII had closed all the monasteries (see Part 3).

SOURCE 20

A cartoon of a 'patentee' or monopolist, 1624.

The **Commons** were becoming an important part of Parliament. When the Crown wanted to raise taxes it had to ask the Commons before it asked the **Lords**, not after. Also, both the Commons and the Lords had to agree to new laws. It had once been just the Lords who needed to do this.

A member of the Commons, called the Speaker, chaired their discussions. The Commons were supposed to choose their Speaker; but he was always someone the monarch thought suitable.

The Commons were called the Lower House. The Lords, the Upper House, were still the senior part of Parliament and sat in the Parliament House itself. It had a bar, or rail, across one end and the Commons were not allowed beyond it (source 19).

Although Parliament was more important in 1500 than it had been before, it existed only to serve the Crown and it stayed that way for the next 140 years. It met only when the monarch called it, and the members went home when they were ordered to. Henry VII called Parliament five times in the first ten years of his reign because he needed its help. After that he hardly called it at all. Henry VIII called it nine times in thirty-seven years. Elizabeth I called it ten times during her forty-five-year reign.

Statutes

By the middle of the sixteeenth century, people agreed that statutes, the laws made by Parliament, were the most powerful laws in the land. This was because a statute needed the agreement of the Crown and of both houses of Parliament, which stood for all the people of England and Wales.

Freedom of speech

The Commons had to advise the monarch. But, what happened if the king or queen did not like what they said or the way they said it? In the sixteenth century the Speaker started to ask the monarch to allow members to offer advice without having to worry that the monarch might think them rude or critical.

The monarch always agreed to this 'freedom of speech' for the Commons. But it was a freedom to talk about the things the monarch wanted advice about, not to discuss any subject the Commons chose.

The Commons advises the Crown

Towards the end of the sixteenth century the Crown was short of money. As well as asking Parliament to agree to more taxes, Elizabeth I raised extra money in other ways. One was to give a royal grant, in return for a sum of money, which allowed someone to be the only person who could make or sell a certain item. The grant was called a 'patent' and the privilege it gave was called a 'monopoly' (source 20).

activity

1 Look at sources 20–22. Make a list of reasons why you think people hated monopolies.
2 What does this episode tell you about **a** the Commons in 1601, **b** Elizabeth I in 1601?

Monopolies were very unpopular, so in 1597 the Commons complained about them. Elizabeth promised not to grant so many, but she carried on just the same. At the next Parliament, in 1601, a member complained:

SOURCE 21

These patentees are worse than ever they were . . . These are now in being . . . the patents for currants, iron, powder, cards, horns, . . . bottles, glasses, bags, . . . aniseed, vinegar, . . . steel . . . brushes, pots, salt, saltpetre, lead, oil, . . . and divers [many] others.

Hayward Townshend, *Historical Collections*, printed 1680

Hearing this list, the next speaker stood up and said:

SOURCE 22

Is not bread there? . . . If order be not taken for [if something isn't done about] these, bread will be there before the next Parliament.

Hayward Townshend, *Historical Collections*, printed 1680

When she heard how angry the Commons were, Elizabeth sent a message to say she would cancel some patents immediately and look in to the rest. She thanked them for their advice. The Commons were pleased that at last she had listened to them.

assignments

1 Look at source 4. Imagine you are the Venetian ambassador to London in the time of Elizabeth. Use the evidence in sources 13–16 to write a report telling the rulers of Venice about her.

2a Make a list of the sorts of information that you can get about the Crown and government by looking at (i) sources 8 and 14, (ii) sources 2 and 16.
b Do you think drawings and paintings made at the time, or written sources are more useful for finding out about the Crown and government? Give your reasons.

3 Use the information and sources on pages 19–21 to make a chart or display to show **a** what changed, and **b** what stayed the same in the relationship of the House of Commons to (i) the Lords, (ii) the Crown.

4 Use source 12 and the sources and information on pages 14–21. Imagine you are a landowner living in the time of Elizabeth I. You decide you want to help to govern the country.
a Think about what you would have to do and what privileges you would have in each of the following positions:
(i) Justice of the Peace; (ii) Member of the House of Commons; (iii) Member of the House of Lords; (iv) Courtier.
b Decide which of these positions you think would give you the most power. Explain your reasons.

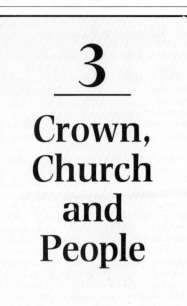

3

Crown, Church and People

A time of change

In 1500 the English accepted that even though the King was their ruler, the Pope in Rome was the head of the Church. By the time James I became king in 1603, this had changed. The King, not the Pope, was head of the English Church, which was now the 'Church of England'. Many people thought the Pope and Roman Catholics – those who still followed the old Church – were enemies of England. In Part 3 you can work out for yourself why these changes happened.

Henry VIII's divorce

Sometime before 1525, Henry VIII started to worry because his only surviving child was a girl, Mary, and his wife, Catherine of Aragon, was getting too old to have any more children. Some people thought a woman could not succeed to the throne. Henry wanted a male heir.

Shortly afterwards he fell passionately in love with a young woman at Court called Anne Boleyn who refused to become his lover unless he promised to marry her. If Henry could end his marriage to Catherine, he might solve both his problems at once.

Although the Church did not normally allow divorce, the Pope had the power to annul, or end, a marriage. In Henry's case, Pope Clement VII refused. In the end, helped by his minister Thomas Cromwell, Henry used Parliament to pass a law which said that the English Church could decide about the divorce without the Pope.

When the Archbishop of Canterbury died, Henry appointed a new one, Thomas Cranmer, who was prepared to hold a Church court which announced that Catherine and Henry had an **unlawful marriage**. If Henry had never been married properly to Catherine in the first place, he was free to marry Anne.

Anne was already pregnant when she and Henry married in 1533. Their baby was a girl, Elizabeth.

> **i** **Unlawful marriage** *The Book of Leviticus in the Bible says that a man may not marry the widow of his brother. Catherine had first married Henry's older brother, Arthur, who died. The Pope then gave Henry special permission to marry Catherine. Despite this, Henry said his marriage to her was unlawful and Cranmer's court agreed.*

> **i** **Woodcut** *A print made by cutting away wood from a block to leave a design. This is then covered with ink and printed. Woodcuts first appeared in Europe in the early 15th century. When the printing press was invented they were used as book illustrations.*

The break with Rome

Henry had disobeyed the Pope. Now he and Cromwell had to make sure the Pope could not reverse the decision over the divorce. In 1534 Parliament passed a law which said that:

SOURCE 1

The king our soveriegn lord, his heirs and successors . . . shall be taken, accepted and reputed [considered] the only supreme head in earth of the Church of England . . .

Act of Supremacy, 1534

SOURCE 2

The Pope suppressed by Henry VIII, a **woodcut** made at the time of Henry's break with Rome. Henry is shown with his feet resting on the Pope's back.

The closing of the monasteries

SOURCE 3

The ruins of Rievaulx Abbey, North Yorkshire, a Cistercian monastery founded in 1131. The monks here were skilled in farming, wool production and crafts such as pottery.

Many European rulers were angry about Henry's treatment of both the Pope and Catherine (she was the king of Spain's aunt). Henry expected to be attacked by France, Germany, Scotland and Spain. He needed money to defend the country.

With Cromwell's help, he persuaded Parliament that monks, nuns and friars were lazy, immoral and more interested in making money than in serving God. Laws were passed to close all monasteries. Royal officials took them over and sold off their lands to raise money for the Crown.

The only serious resistance came from the north of England, where about 40,000 people joined a rebellion known as the Pilgrimage of Grace. The rebel leader, Robert Aske, said he opposed the closures because:

SOURCE 4

The abbeys in the north parts gave great alms [charitable gifts] to poor men and laudably [worthily] served God . . . Also the abbeys were one of the beauties of this realm to all men . . . They educated boys . . . and nunneries brought girls up in virtue [to lead good lives] . . . Monks maintained sea-walls, bridges and highways . . .

From the examination of Robert Aske, 1537

The rebels went home when Henry promised to save their monasteries. Then he had the leaders hanged and closed the monasteries anyway.

activity

1 How does source 3 show that the monasteries were wealthy?

2 Use source 4 to make a list of services performed by monks and nuns that were ended by the closure of the monasteries.

3 What reasons did Henry give Parliament for closing the monasteries? What other reasons did he have?

4 Make a list of the different sorts of people you think were most badly affected by the closure of the monasteries.

The Protestant reformers

Even before Henry broke away from Rome, some English people were interested in the ideas of Protestant reformers in other European countries. They were called 'Protestants' because they were protesting against the Church, and 'reformers' because they wanted to reform, or change, it.

The Church treated them as **heretics** and ordered many of them to be burnt (source 5). In the end Protestants set up their own churches. The members of the original Church are known as 'Roman Catholics' or just 'Catholics'. Two important Protestant reformers were Martin Luther and John Calvin.

SOURCE 5

The title page of the 1641 edition of a book first published in 1563 shows the Protestant point of view. The Protestants are on the left. Find them:
- listening to the preacher
- reading and discussing the Bible
- being burnt at the stake for their opinions
- wearing crowns in Heaven and praising God with the angels.

The Catholics are on the right. Find them:
- listening to a priest
- going in procession to a shrine
- worshipping the bread at the **Mass** round the altar
- in hell with demons.

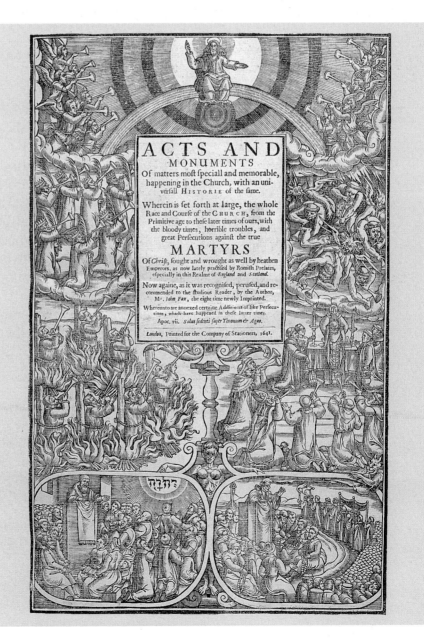

i **Mass** *The Catholic Church's most important service. The priest repeated the actions of Christ at the Last Supper by eating bread and drinking wine, and the people shared the wine. The Church taught that at a particular point in the service the bread and the wine miraculously became the body and blood of Christ and that those who received them became united with Christ at that moment.*

Martin Luther

Luther was a German friar who taught religion at Wittenberg University. He became particularly angry when, in 1517, another friar, John Tetzel, arrived in Germany from Rome saying God would forgive the sins of anyone who paid him a sum of money. The money was to be used to build the new St Peter's Church in Rome.

Luther thought hard about what a person really needed to do in order to earn God's forgiveness and go to Heaven. He decided that what mattered most was to believe truly in Jesus Christ. This was more important than going to lots of Masses or making pilgrimages.

Luther and his followers said that if people were truly to understand about Christ, they had to be able to read the Bible for themselves. That meant it had to be translated into their own language from Latin.

John Calvin

Calvin was a French priest who founded his own church in Geneva in Switzerland. He thought the most important job of a priest was to preach and teach (source 6).

There were no crosses in his churches, no candles and no pictures of Jesus and the saints. Calvinist priests wore plain gowns in church instead of the robes worn by Catholic priests.

The Catholic Church taught that when the priest blessed the bread and the wine during the Mass, they miraculously became the body and blood of Christ. Calvin said they did not. He argued that according to the Bible they simply represented Christ's body and blood.

In Calvin's church the members of each parish elected their own priest who was called a 'presbyter'. That is why Calvinists are often known as Presbyterians.

activity

Work in pairs.
1 Look at source 6 and the information in the text. Make a list of the differences between the inside of this church and the inside of a Catholic church.
2 Look at source 5 and the information in the text.
a Make a list of the things the Catholics are shown doing.
b Imagine one of you is a sixteenth-century follower of Calvin and the other a Catholic. What would (i) the Calvinist, (ii) the Catholic say about the things the Catholics are doing?

SOURCE 6

Calvinists at worship in Lyon, France. A sixteenth-century painting.

The English Church, 1540–1603

Although Henry VIII quarrelled with the Pope, he did not wish to change any of the things the Church told people they should believe. But, within ten years of his death, people were divided over what kind of church the English Church should be (source 7).

SOURCE 7

Changes in the English Church, 1540–1603.

Henry VIII

1534
Act of Supremacy made the Crown the 'Supreme Head' of the Church of England.

1539
The Great Bible published in English.

Mary I

1553
Pope restored as head of the English Church. All changes made by Edward VI cancelled.

1554
Law passed to make Protestantism a heresy.

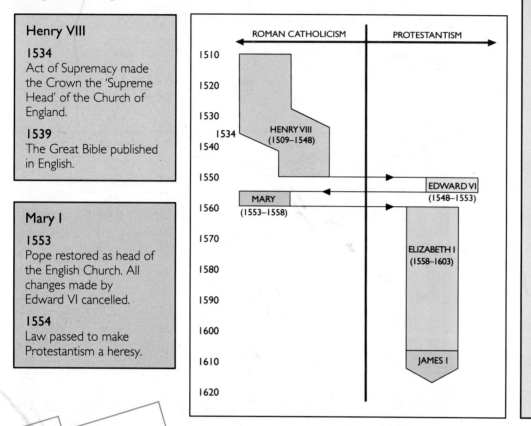

Edward VI

1549
Cranmer's First Prayer Book, consisting of the usual Church services, translated from Latin into English.

1549
Priests allowed to marry. In the north of England about one in ten were married by 1553, and in London about one in three.

1552
Cranmer's Second Prayer Book. He left out the Mass and put in a 'communion' service in which the bread and wine represented Christ's body and blood. Also, priests were told to wear a simple white linen garment, called a surplice, instead of their usual robes and to replace stone altars with wooden communion tables.

activity

1 Look at source 7. What changes **a** inside the local church, **b** in church services would an ordinary villager have noticed in (i) 1549, (ii) 1552, (iii) 1553, (iv) 1559? Give reasons for your answers.

ⓘ **Welsh Bible** *The translation was by William Morgan, helped by several others. Morgan was a Welshman with strongly Protestant views. He became Bishop of Llandaff in 1595. The Bible helped the spread of Protestant ideas in Wales. It also encouraged people to write other books in Welsh. People from all social classes in Wales spoke Welsh until about 1700. After that some landowners and priests started to speak mainly English.*

Elizabeth I

1559
Act of Supremacy made the Crown the 'Supreme Governor' of the Church of England.

Act of Uniformity ordered everyone to use a new Prayer Book based on those of 1549 and 1552. The words for the communion service were carefully written to allow Catholics to believe the bread and wine turned into the body and blood of Christ, and Protestants to believe they were just a symbol.

A new law said everyone had to go to church on Sunday.

Parliament ordered the Bible and Prayer Book to be translated into Welsh. Welsh Prayer Book published in 1567 and **Welsh Bible** in 1588.

Edward VI (1547–53) was strongly Protestant and wanted a Protestant Church. Mary (1553–58) was strongly Catholic and wanted everything to be as it had been before Henry VIII broke away from Rome. It was left to Elizabeth (1558–1603) to try to put an end to religious arguments. She favoured a Protestant Church, but above all she wanted a united country and church services which everyone could go to. Her religious settlement was an attempt to create a Church of England which as many people as possible could support.

Why did Catholics become so unpopular?

Elizabeth knew that many people still believed in the Catholic faith and did not like Protestant ideas. Ordinary people had been pleased when Mary succeeded Edward VI because they knew she would bring back the Catholic services with which they were familiar.

Even though Elizabeth wanted people to accept a more Protestant Church, it took a very long time for them to do so. In 1569 a bishop in Sussex wrote:

SOURCE 8

They have . . . in many places images hidden . . . and other popish [Catholic] ornaments, ready to set up the Mass again at twenty-four hours warning . . .

A report by Bishop Barlow of Chichester on Sussex parishes, 1569

In 1595 at least a fifth of the Justices of the Peace in Sussex were Catholics. Most Welsh people were still Catholic at this time, as well as many in the north of England. This is not really surprising when you think how long Catholic beliefs had been the official beliefs of the Church.

Most of these Catholics were loyal to the Crown and simply wished to worship in their own way. Yet, by James I's reign, many people thought of them as dangerous traitors. In the rest of Part 3 you can work out why this happened.

Protestant martyrs

Although many people were pleased that Mary stood for the traditional Roman Catholic Church with the Pope at its head, they were horrified by the way she allowed Protestants to be treated.

When Mary became queen, about 800 Protestants left the country to live in exile, mainly in Germany and Geneva. Many of those who stayed behind were accused of heresy and, if they did not publicly change their beliefs, they were burnt.

The stories of their trials and deaths were collected by John Foxe, one of the exiles, and published in 1563 in a book called *The Acts and Monuments*, but which was known as Foxe's Book of Martyrs (source 9).

SOURCE 9

The burning of Bishops Latimer and Ridley at Oxford, October 1555. From Foxe's Book of Martyrs, 1563. Foxe wanted to show the suffering and heroism of the Protestants and the cruelty of their Catholic persecutors. His book was so successful that it influenced English people's opinions against Catholics for well over a hundred years.

SOURCE 10

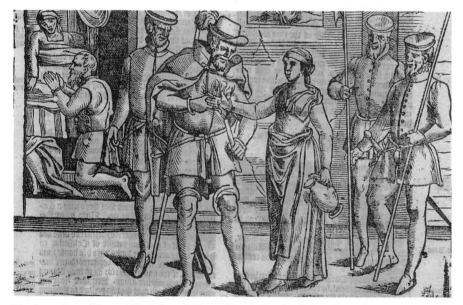

The burning of Rose Allin's hand. From Foxe's Book of Martyrs, 1563.

activity

1 How do you think Mary's treatment of Protestants helped to make Catholics unpopular?

2 Look at sources 9–12. Why do you think Foxe's book was so successful?

Most of those burnt for heresy were ordinary people like Rose Allin (source 10). Foxe told how a man called Tyrrel went to arrest Rose's mother and stepfather on suspicion of being Protestants. Her mother was ill in bed and asked Rose to fetch a drink.

When Rose returned, carrying a jar of water in one hand and a candle in the other, Tyrrel accused her of heresy:

SOURCE 11

Then that cruel Tyrrel, taking the candle from her, held her wrist, and the burning candle under her hand, burning cross-wise over the back thereof so long till the very sinews [tendons] cracked asunder : . . He said often to her, 'Why whore! Wilt thou not cry?' . . .

From John Foxe, *The Acts and Monuments*, 1563

Later, in prison, Rose told a friend:

SOURCE 12

While my one hand was . . . a-burning, I, having a pot in my other hand, might have laid him on the face with it . . . But I thank God with all my heart, I did it not.

From John Foxe, *The Acts and Monuments*, 1563

The whole family was found guilty of heresy and burnt.

Catholic plots

Some Catholics were not loyal to the Crown and plotted to get rid of Elizabeth. Because of this it became more and more difficult for the government to trust any Catholics.

Mary Queen of Scots

Abdicate To give up the throne so that someone else can rule instead.

Some Catholics believed Mary Stuart, Queen of Scots, as a great-granddaughter of Henry VII, had a better claim to the throne than Elizabeth (Part 1, source 9). Although Mary was a Catholic herself, Scotland's Church had been Protestant since 1560. In 1568 Mary was forced to **abdicate** so that her Protestant son, James, could rule instead.

She escaped to England and asked Elizabeth for protection. Elizabeth decided to keep her under guard until she could go back to Scotland. That time never came and, instead, Mary became the centre of a series of Catholic plots against Elizabeth. Finally, after yet another plot to kill Elizabeth was discovered in 1586, Mary was accused of being involved. She was tried, found guilty, and executed in 1587.

activity

1 Why do you think the government treated Catholic priests as traitors?

Pope and priests

In 1570 the Pope excommunicated Elizabeth. This meant that she was no longer a member of the Catholic Church and so English Catholics no longer had to obey her. Instead they were supposed to support rebellions against her.

Then, in 1580, English and Welsh Catholics who had trained abroad as priests started to return secretly to spread Catholicism. They claimed to be loyal to the Crown, but those that were caught were executed as traitors.

Foreign threats

When Mary Tudor was queen, she married Prince Philip, heir to the Spanish throne, who eventually became King Philip II of Spain. This was not a popular move. Spain was a Catholic country, but even some English Catholics were unhappy that England might eventually fall under Spanish control.

Fear of foreign interference grew even worse under Elizabeth. Throughout her reign people were concerned that either France or Spain might attack England to try to restore Catholicism.

While Mary Queen of Scots was alive, Philip II of Spain was content to wait and see if any plots succeeded in removing Elizabeth. Once she was dead, he decided to invade England himself. In 1588 he ordered a fleet of warships, the mighty Spanish Armada, to set sail.

As the Armada sailed down the English Channel, the militia gathered at Tilbury near London, ready to meet the expected invasion. Elizabeth's advisers told her not to go near large groups of armed people, for fear of assassination by Catholics. But she insisted on going there and speaking to the troops:

SOURCE 13

Let tyrants fear. I have always . . . placed my chiefest strength and safeguard in the loyal hearts and good will of my subjects . . . Therefore I am come amongst you as you see . . . being resolved in the midst and heat of the battle, to live or die amongst you all, and to lay down for my God and for my kingdom and for my people, my honour and my blood, even in the dust.

I know I have the body of a weak and feeble woman, but I have the heart and stomach of a king, and of a king of England too, and I think foul scorn that . . . any prince of Europe should dare to invade the borders of my realm . . .

Elizabeth I's speech to her troops at Tilbury, 18 or 19 August, 1588

activity

2 What can you learn from source 13 about:
a the Catholic threat;
b Elizabeth's attitude to it;
c her skills as a ruler?

In the end the militia was not needed. The Armada was defeated at sea, partly by the English navy and partly by storms which eventually wrecked it. Elizabeth had a medal made to commemorate the victory. The Latin words on it said:

SOURCE 14

God blew, and they were scattered.

Commemorative medal, 1588

The portrait of Elizabeth which was painted to celebrate the defeat of the Spaniards (source 15) took up the idea that God was on the side of Protestant England against the Catholic enemy. Through one window in the back, you can see the Armada; through the other, the storm God sent to wreck it.

SOURCE 15

The Armada portrait of Elizabeth I, painted between 1588 and 1592.

The spread of Protestant beliefs

Although many people hung on to their traditional Catholic beliefs, Protestant ideas spread steadily. Some Protestants wanted to get rid of everything that reminded them of the Catholic Church. They wanted to purify the Church and because of this they became known as 'Puritans'.

Puritans (source 16) thought it was important to read and discuss the Bible. They wanted educated ministers who could preach good sermons. They disliked ceremony in church services and wanted ministers to dress simply, not in robes. They thought Sunday should be a day for religious worship and Bible study, so they disapproved of people playing sports and games after church.

activity

1 How does source 16 suggest that Puritans thought
a family life,
b hard work,
c education
were important?

SOURCE 16

A Puritan family painted in the middle of the seventeenth century.

James I and the Catholics

SOURCE 17

The Double Deliverance, a cartoon engraved by Samuel Ward in 1621. Find:
- Guy Fawkes (a member of the Gunpowder Plot) walking towards Parliament House, which has barrels of gunpowder in the cellar
- the Pope, the Devil and the King of Spain in a tent, plotting against England
- the Spanish Armada.

Two years into the reign of James I, Catholics were involved in yet another plot. This was the Gunpowder Plot of 1605, a failed attempt to blow up the Parliament House when the King would be in it.

In 1621 James I planned to marry his son, Charles, to the infanta, the daughter of the king of Spain. He thought this would help to bring Catholics and Protestants together and give peace to Europe. Most English people violently disagreed. A Puritan minister called Samuel Ward engraved a cartoon (source 17) to persuade people that Catholics were never to be trusted. It showed God saving England from the Spanish Armada and the Gunpowder Plot. In the end, Charles did not marry the infanta.

activity

2 Source 17 is a piece of propaganda against Catholics. Many English Catholics were loyal to the Crown and simply wished to worship in the traditional way. Design a poster to persuade seventeenth-century people of their point of view.

assignments

I Some things in the religious life of England and Wales in 1600 were very different from the way they had been in 1500. Some were the same.

a Use words, pictures and diagrams to make a display to show those things which were (i) the same, (ii) different.

b Look at the things that were different. Which ones do you think changed (i) rapidly, (ii) gradually? Write a few sentences to explain your reasons in each case.

c Take those things in **a** that were different by 1600. Some changes make life worse; some make it better. When things improve we call this progress. Who out of (i) Henry VIII, (ii) John Foxe, (iii) Mary Tudor would describe those differences as 'progress'? Who would not? Explain your reasons.

2 During the sixteenth and early seventeenth centuries, Catholics became increasingly unpopular in England.

a Use the sources and information in Part 3 to make lists of (i) some of the causes of this change, (ii) some of its consequences.

b Which (i) cause, (ii) consequence do you think was the most important? Explain your reasons.

3a Use the evidence in sources 9, 10, 11 and 12 to make lists of words that you think describe the actions of (i) Catholics, (ii) Protestants.

b Do the Protestants or the Catholics come out of this best?

c Is this what Foxe intended?

d To what extent do you think you can rely on the evidence of the Book of Martyrs to tell you about the attitudes of (i) Catholics, (ii) Protestants?

The power of the Crown

When Henry VIII succeeded to the throne in 1509 he became King of England and Wales and Lord of Ireland. But the Crown was not equally powerful in each of these places. The further away from London you were, the less power it had.

During the sixteenth and early seventeenth centuries, the Crown tried to increase its power in Wales and Ireland. You can find out about this in Part 4 and decide for yourself how successful you think it was.

You can also find out about Scotland, where the Crown also increased its power during the sixteenth century. It was a Scottish king, James VI (source 1), who in 1603 united the Crowns of Scotland and England.

SOURCE 1

James VI of Scotland and I of England, painted in 1621. He was descended from Henry VII and Elizabeth of York (see source 4, Part 1). The English invited him to be their king when Queen Elizabeth died in 1603. Although he united the crowns of both countries, they remained separate kingdoms with their own parliaments.

activity

1 Use the sources and information in the text to make a list of all the ways in which the power of the Crown in Wales was greater in 1543 than it had been in 1485.
2 Which Welsh people probably (i) supported these changes, (ii) did not? Give your reasons.

Wales

When Henry VII became king, Wales was divided into two separate regions (source 2). The lands conquered by Edward I in the thirteenth century were divided into shires and known as the Principality, because they were ruled by the king's eldest child – the Prince or Princess of Wales.

The remaining lands were divided into Marcher lordships which, until recently, had been ruled by almost independent barons. By 1485 many Marcher lordships belonged to the Crown, but they were still governed differently from the lands in the Principality. The laws were Welsh, not English, and many local landowners kept special rights and privileges.

Even in the Principality, Welsh landowners liked to take the law into their own hands. Henry VII used the Council of Wales to help to

SOURCE 2

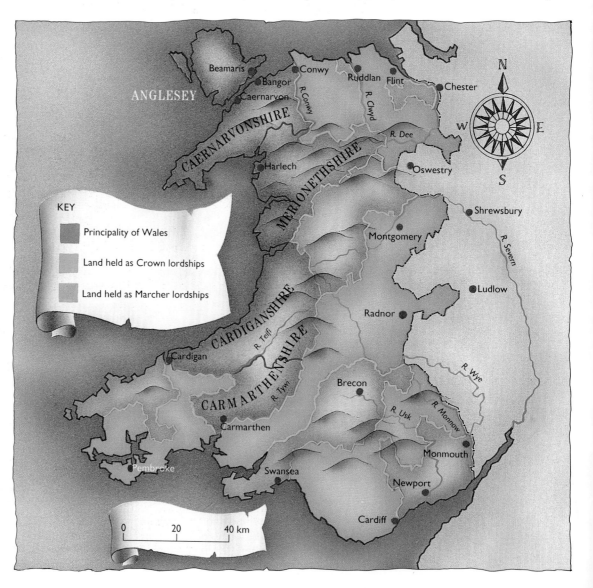

KEY

Principality of Wales

Land held as Crown lordships

Land held as Marcher lordships

Wales in the time of Henry VII.

SOURCE 3

Wales after the
Act of Union,
1536.

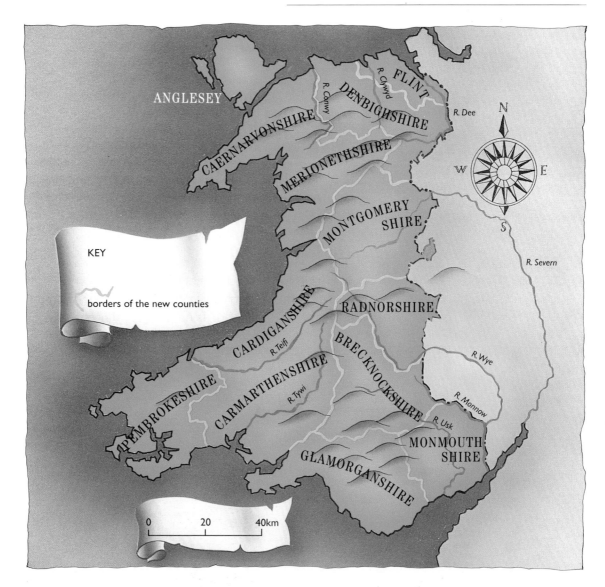

rule the Principality and the Crown lands in the Marches. In 1534
Parliament made a law giving the Council power to supervise justice
in the Marcher Lordships. In 1536 it passed the Act of Union which:

- took away nearly all the powers of the Marcher lords
- allowed the King to divide the Marcher lordships into shires
  (source 3)
- abolished the use of Welsh law and replaced it with English law
  throughout Wales
- gave the Welsh the right to elect MPs
- allowed people to continue speaking the Welsh language

Another Act introduced Justices of the Peace into Welsh shires for
the first time. They were chosen from among Welsh **gentry** who
were pleased to have the chance to govern in their localities.

In 1543 a second Act of Union put the whole of Wales under the
supervision of the Council of Wales and set up travelling law courts
called 'Great Sessions' which carried out the same job as Courts of
Assize in England.

i **Gentry** *The name given
to well-off landowners
who were not lords.*

Ireland

Land and people

Ireland was divided into two worlds – one Gaelic, one English. These usually corresponded to the areas of Irish and English lordship (source 4), though in some parts the two worlds mixed.

The Irish lordships

The Irish lordships formed a Gaelic-speaking world with Gaelic laws and customs. They were ruled by Gaelic lords who were often at war, either with English lords or with rival members of their own family.

SOURCE 4

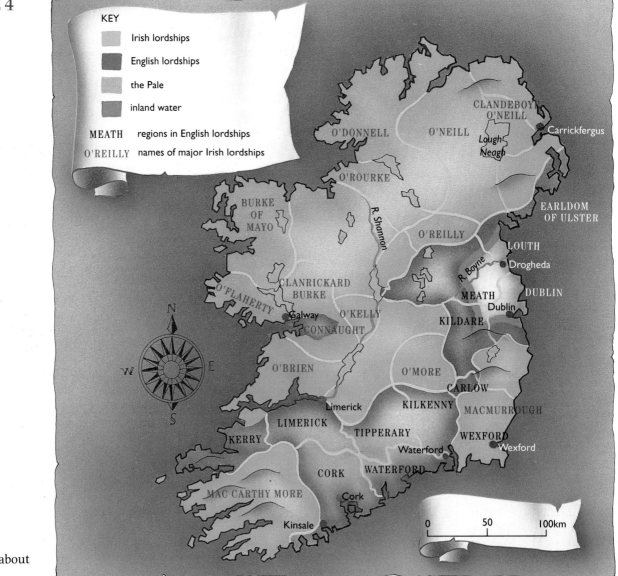

KEY

Irish lordships

English lordships

the Pale

inland water

MEATH   regions in English lordships

O'REILLY   names of major Irish lordships

Ireland in about 1534.

i **Bards**   *Poets who made their living by praising the deeds of the Gaelic lords.*

Each lord appointed a 'brehon', or judge, whose job was to make sure anyone committing a crime gave money or goods to the victim as compensation. Brehons came from educated families who often ran schools to teach Gaelic law. **Bards** also ran schools to teach the rules of Irish verse and the art of composing poems.

People lived mainly by farming herds of cattle and sheep, often moving with their animals to find new pastures.

The English lordships

The English lords were descended from the Norman-English barons who had conquered Ireland in the Middle Ages. They called themselves the 'Old English'.

The English world, where people lived by English laws and spoke English, was strongest in the area around Dublin known as the 'Pale'. English lordships outside the Pale were often affected by the Gaelic world. Members of English and Gaelic ruling families married one another. Many Gaelic-speaking people lived in the countryside of the English lordships and often people lived by a mixture of Gaelic and English law.

Towns and trade

Most Irish towns were self-governing. Townspeople spoke English and followed English laws. They traded with the people of the countryside and then sold the goods to merchants in England, Scotland, France and Spain.

They sold cowhides, sheepskins, furs and woollen cloth. They also sold fish such as salmon and herring. In return they bought wine, salt, iron, pottery and metal goods.

The Crown

Although the English king claimed to be Lord of Ireland, the Crown was powerful only in the Pale (source 4) and some other English lordships. Several Old English lords were almost independent. Gaelic lords recognised the Crown as their overlord, but they too ruled independently.

The king governed through a Lord Deputy based in Dublin who was helped by a Council and a Parliament. Lords and bishops from all over Ireland were supposed to attend Parliament, as well as representatives from all towns, and from shires in the English lordships. However, the only people who attended Parliament regularly came from the Pale.

There were Justices of the Peace in the Pale and some English lordships outside it. Judges from Dublin travelled round to hold Courts of Assize.

activity

1 Look at source 4 and the information in the text. Make three maps of Ireland using colours to show where you think the power of:
a the Irish lords;
b the Old English lords;
c the Crown was (i) strong, (ii) medium, (iii) weak.

activity

Work in pairs.
1 Look at source 7.
a How would the life of an Irish family living in an Irish lordship change after 1541 if Henry VIII had his way?
b What do you think the family might think about this? Explain your reasons.

The Crown increases control

After Henry VIII's break with Rome, the Irish Parliament declared that he was:

SOURCE 5

The only supreme head in earth of the whole Church in Ireland.

Act of Irish Parliament, 1536

But Henry knew some Gaelic lords believed the Pope, not the English king, had the right to be called Lord of Ireland. So in 1541 Parliament enacted:

SOURCE 6

That the king's highness, his heirs and successors, kings of England, be always kings of this land of Ireland.

Act of Irish Parliament, 1541

Henry said he wanted the Irish to become:

SOURCE 7

True subjects, obedient to his laws, foresaking [giving up] their Irish laws, habits and customs.

State Papers, 1541

From then on, Lord Deputies tried to make the Irish follow English rather than Gaelic law; speak English not Gaelic; and even wear clothes of the English fashion.

The Lord Deputies gradually managed to control the south and east, and Ireland was re-organised into counties (source 8); but the northern area, known as Ulster, remained strongly Gaelic.

In 1595 the Earl of Tyrone was offered the lordship of O'Neill. This was an ancient Gaelic royal title and the Crown had forbidden its use. Tyrone saw a chance to become leader of Gaelic Ireland and accepted the title. So, Elizabeth I sent an army against him.

Old English lords in the south, who were Catholics and also felt the Crown was taking away their traditional authority, decided to support him. The king of Spain sent him 3,500 troops. After a bitter war, Tyrone surrendered in 1603. The Crown had finally managed to conquer the whole of Ireland.

James I's government borrowed a Tudor idea and carried out the 'plantation' of Ulster. Plantation means settlement by colonists. The government thought the Irish were dangerous, because they were Catholics, and uncivilised, because of their Gaelic way of life. Its plan was to encourage Protestant settlers to colonise areas of Ireland in the hope that their religious beliefs and way of life would to rub off on the Irish people and change them for the better.

SOURCE 8

Ireland in 1603, and Tudor and early Stuart Plantations.

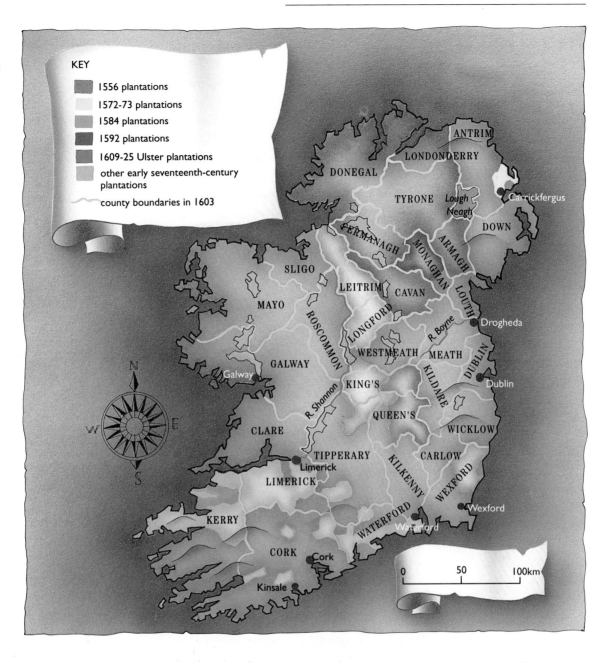

KEY

- 1556 plantations
- 1572-73 plantations
- 1584 plantations
- 1592 plantations
- 1609-25 Ulster plantations
- other early seventeenth-century plantations
- county boundaries in 1603

activity

2 Look at source 8 and the information in the text. The government hoped the Irish might eventually take up the beliefs and way of life of the Protestant settlers. Make a list of reasons why you think that did not happen.

3 Look at source 9 and the information in the text. Write the speech an Old English lord might have made in reply to James I.

First the government put Protestants in the place of Gaelic landlords. Then the new landlords arranged for more Protestants from England and Scotland to settle on the lands of the Irish, who had to move to smaller plots of land to make room (source 8).

The Old English soon started to complain that the government listened only to the newcomers, the 'New English'. They claimed that they could be Catholics and still be loyal the Crown; but James I called them 'half-subjects', saying:

SOURCE 9

You give your soul to the Pope and to me only the body and even it . . . you divide between me and the king of Spain . . . Strive . . . to become good subjects . . . and then I shall respect you all alike.

James I's speech to the Old English delegation, 21 April 1614

Scotland

Land and people

SOURCE 10

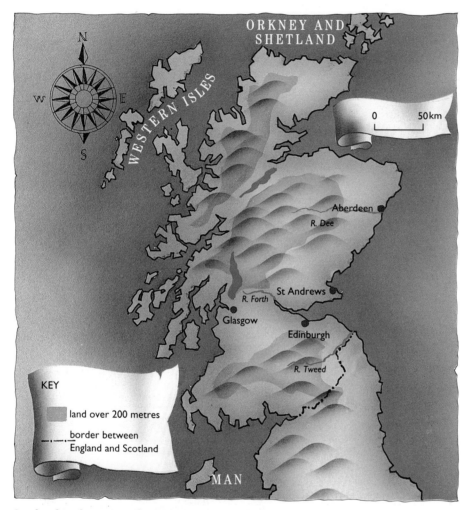

Scotland in the sixteenth century.

Sixteenth-century Scotland was a poor country. There were some towns, but most Scots lived by farming land which they rented from a lord. Several families lived in separate huts on one farm and shared the work. They grew corn and owned a few animals.

Like the Irish, the Scots produced mainly raw materials such as wool, cowhides and furs. They also had fish to sell, especially salmon and herring. They had to buy a lot from abroad because very few things were made at home.

Scottish merchants traded in England, France, Spain, the Netherlands and the lands around the Baltic. One of them kept a list of the things sent home from the Netherlands, and their cost:

SOURCE 11

	£	s	d
Sent to Janet Patterson			
3 pieces of chequered cloth	2	11	0
50lb of rice		7	0
17lb of pepper		19	0
Sent to Sir Robert Wells			
A Spanish sword		19	6
A little tin of ginger		7	6
Half a **ream** of paper		1	6
A bag		4	4
Sent to the Duke of Ross			
125 **ells** of linen cloth	3	2	6
4 feather beds	4	0	0
3 dozen pewter dishes and 3 **chargers**	9	14	9

From Andrew Halyburton's ledger, 1492–1503

Although Scotland was poor, the Scots impressed the Spanish ambassador:

SOURCE 12

The people are handsome. They like foreigners so much that they dispute [argue] with one another as to who shall have . . . a foreigner in his house. They are vain . . . They spend all they have to keep up appearances. They are as well dressed as is possible to be in such a country . . . They are courageous, strong, quick and agile.

Don Pedro d'Ayala, *Description of Scotland*, 1498

Education and learning

After the wars with England in the Middle Ages, Scots stopped going to the universities of Oxford and Cambridge. Instead they founded their own universities at St Andrews (1411), Glasgow (1451) and Aberdeen (1495). People usually went on from these to study in other European universities such as Paris in France, Cologne in Germany and Bologna in Italy.

When the Pope wrote to King James IV agreeing to the foundation of Aberdeen University, he said:

SOURCE 13

In the northerly parts of the kingdom there are some places separated from the rest of the realm by arms of the sea and very steep mountains, in which regions dwell men who are uncultivated and ignorant of letters [learning].

Bull of Pope Alexander VI, 1495

activity

1 How is source 11 evidence that **a** the Scots did not make very many things themselves, **b** some Scots could afford luxuries?
2 Look at sources 10 and 13.
a What, according to the Pope, are the differences between the northerly parts of Scotland and the rest?
b How does this help to explain the choice of Aberdeen as the site for a new university?

The Crown

The Stuart kings of Scotland governed with the help of a Council and a Parliament called the Three Estates. Here lords, bishops and representatives of the people sat together in one place – unlike England where Parliament was divided into the separate Houses of Lords and Commons.

SOURCE 14

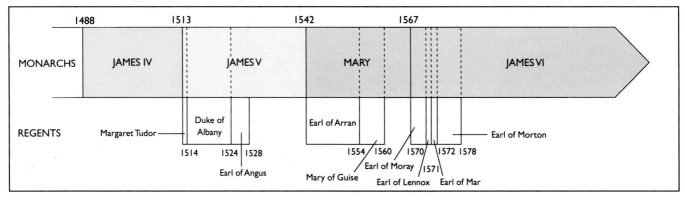

Rulers of Scotland in the sixteenth century.

Like Henry VIII in England, James IV was a new kind of king, interested in new ideas and the work of artists and architects. The Spanish ambassador wrote that:

SOURCE 15

He is courageous, even more than a king should be . . . I have often seen him undertake most dangerous things . . . He speaks . . . Latin, very well, French, German, Flemish, Italian and Spanish . . . He is well read in the bible and . . . other devout books.

Don Pedro d'Ayala, *Description of Scotland*, 1498

James founded the Scottish Royal College of Surgeons as well as Aberdeen University. He also ordered all barons and freeholders to send their eldest sons to school to learn Latin and law:

SOURCE 16

So that they may have knowledge and understanding of the laws . . . so that they that are Sheriffs or Judges . . . may have knowledge to do justice.

Act of Parliament, 1496

Stuart kings rarely fought wars, so they could afford to spend money on splendid tournaments, and impressive ships (source 17) and buildings (source 18). They wanted to be thought of as important monarchs in Europe.

SOURCE 17

A model of James IV's ship the 'Great Michael'.

activity

1 Look at the sources and information on pages 8–13 and pages 44–47.
a In what ways were James IV of Scotland and Henry VIII of England similar as kings?
b Can you suggest some differences?

SOURCE 18

The south range of Falkland Palace, built by James V, the son of James IV, who ruled Scotland 1513–42.

James VI and I: different interpretations

In 1603 James VI accepted the English invitation to become their king. So he became James VI of Scotland and James I of England.

James was very successful as king of Scotland. He managed to control both great lords and Highland chiefs when they showed signs of rebellion. He divided Scotland into four districts and appointed royal judges to visit each district twice a year to hear the cases of criminals brought before them. He invited weavers from the Netherlands to teach Scottish weavers how to make better cloth that would sell abroad. He encouraged gold, silver and coal mining, and tried to get merchants to build bigger ships.

He also managed to protect his power against the claims of the Scottish Church. In 1560 the Scottish Parliament had set up a **Presbyterian** Church, or Kirk, in Scotland. Each parish, or congregation, chose its own priest, called a 'minister', and ministers and elected members from each congregation met in a General Assembly to discuss the Kirk's affairs. Kirk leaders claimed the king was an ordinary member of the Kirk and not its head. They also wanted to get rid of bishops. But James managed to become both head of the Kirk and to keep bishops.

One historian has said of James:

> **i** **Presbyterian** A Presbyterian Church is one in which the members of each parish elect their own priest. It is so called because John Calvin, who first set up this kind of Church in Geneva, called his priests 'presbyters'.

SOURCE 19

Despite ... occasional follies [weaknesses] ... we must recognise ... one of the greatest kings Scotland has ever known.

H. Shapiro, *Scotland in the Days of James VI*, 1970

English historians used to criticise James for being a weak king of England. They said he was a clever man but did not have Elizabeth's skills in dealing with people. They blamed him for giving favourites too much power, spending too much money at court and quarrelling with Parliament. They said he was unpleasant and cowardly:

SOURCE 20

He was lacking in self respect and utterly undignified in ... appearance and conduct. He had 'a big head, slobbering tongue, quilted clothes and rickety legs'. He was so timid the sight of a drawn sword made him ill.

Edwards, *Notes on British History*, 1958

These opinions are based on the writings of people who knew James:

SOURCE 21

King James was the most cowardly man that I ever knew. He could not endure a soldier; to hear of war was death to him and how he tormented himself with fear of some sudden mischief may be proved by his great quilted doublets, pistol-proof.

Sir John Oglander's notebook, mid-seventeenth century

SOURCE 22

He was naturally . . . timid . . . his eyes large, ever rolling after any stranger that came into his presence . . . his tongue too large for his mouth . . . his drink . . . came out into the cup of each side of his mouth . . . He was infinitely inclined to peace, but more out of fear than conscience . . .

Sir Anthony Weldon, *The Court and Character of James I*, 1650

Sir John Oglander (source 21) was a supporter of James's son, Charles I, who wanted to prove that James was responsible for the problems facing Charles when he became king. Sir Anthony Weldon (source 22) did not like James because he did not give him a job he wanted.

Other people who knew James had different opinions:

SOURCE 23

He . . . held very good correspondence with all the princes in Christendom . . . While all the Christian world was in wars, he alone governed his people in peace. He was a most just and good king.

Godfrey Goodman, *The Court of James I*, mid-seventeenth century

Today, historians still have criticisms of James, but they take into account his record as king of Scotland and write differently about his support for peace:

SOURCE 24

James . . . had some admirable traits [qualities]. He was warm-hearted, affectionate and generous, and had a genuine love of peace and dislike of violence.

A. G. R. Smith, *The reign of James VI and I*, 1973

---

activity

I Use the sources and information in the text. What view do they give you of James as king of:
a Scotland;
b England ?
2a What impression of James I and VI do you get from reading sources 22 and 22?
b How does source 23 change your picture of him?
c Which sources has Edwards (source 21) probably used?
3 Look at sources 22 and 23 and the information in the text. Do you think you can rely on what **a** Sir John Oglander,
b Sir Anthony Weldon said about James? Explain your answers.

assignments

1a Use the sources and information in Part 4 to make lists of the ways in which the powers of the Crown in (i) Wales, (ii) Ireland changed between 1500 and 1625.
b Write a short paragraph to describe each change.
c Do you think it is right to say that the power of the Crown in (i) Wales, and (ii) Ireland increased over this time? Were there any ways in which it decreased or stayed the same? Explain your answers.

2a What were the differences between Henry VIII's treatment of Wales (page 39) and Ireland (page 42).
b What reasons can you think of for these differences?

3 Suppose a reporter is able to go back in time from the present to 1625 to make a radio or television documentary about different people's opinions of the changes that have taken place in Ireland since 1541. The reporter decides to interview:
a a Gaelic lord;
b an Irish family in Ulster;
c a New English landowner in Ulster;
d an Old English lord;
e James I.
Write what you think each of them would tell the reporter.

4 Use the sources and information on pages 44–47 to make a display showing the strengths and weaknesses of the kingdom of Scotland in the sixteenth century.

5a What would your view of James VI and I be if you only had sources and information about him as:
 (i) king of Scotland
(ii) king of England?
b Use the sources and information in the text to draw up arguments (i) for, (ii) against the view that James was a weak king.
c Which side do you support? Explain your reasons.
d Sources 21 and 22 say James I was cowardly and afraid of violence.
 (i) Look at source 15. Why would people in the sixteenth century be critical of such a king?
(ii) Why might a modern historian (source 24) be less likely to find fault in him?

5
Four Sorts of People

Between 1500 and 1750 writers described English society as a set of layers or ranks with the most important and influential people at the top and the least important at the bottom. In 1577 a country priest called William Harrison wrote:

SOURCE 1

We divide our people commonly into four sorts.

William Harrison, *The Description of England*, 1577

Part 5 is about these 'four sorts' of people, especially those Harrison called the 'fourth sort', the people in the lowest rank of all. You will be able to investigate why some people got much richer and others much poorer between 1500 and 1650, and look at the changes in the way the government tried to deal with very poor people.

The ranks of society

Source 2 shows how people thought of the ranks of society. A person's rank depended partly on wealth and partly on family background. That is why it was possible for a gentleman to be less well-off than a yeoman, though in time a wealthy yeoman could become thought of as a gentleman.

SOURCE 2

This shows how people thought of the ranks of society in the sixteenth and seventeenth centuries. A woman did not belong to a rank in her own right, but held the rank of her father or husband.

Gentlemen
Included lords at one end of the scale and people from a good family, but with not as much wealth as a yeoman, at the other.

Citizens and burgesses
Townspeople with sufficient wealth to qualify them to stand as town councillors and to help to run the affairs of the town. Also professional people such as priests and lawyers.

Yeomen
Farmers who owned land worth at least 40 shillings a year if rented out to other people. That also meant they could vote for a Member of Parliament.

The fourth sort
Labourers, husbandmen, craftsmen, for example – tailors, shoemakers, carpenters.

Gentlemen

SOURCE 3

Sir Henry Tichborne outside his manor house in Hampshire, giving out free bread to the villagers in 1670. Find:
- the manor house. It was built in the sixteenth century
- Sir Henry and his family
- his servants
- the villagers.

A typical country gentleman (source 3) owned a large house and plenty of land. He needed many servants, so his household provided jobs for local people. According to Harrison, the gentry started to build their houses in a different way in the late sixteenth century:

SOURCE 4

The ancient manors and houses of our gentlemen are yet [still], and for the most part, of strong timber . . . Howbeit [However], such as be lately builded are commonly either of brick or hard stone, or both . . . their rooms large and comely [handsome] . . .

William Harrison, *The Description of England*, 1577

activity

1 What does source 3 tell you about **a** what the villagers thought of Sir Henry Tichborne, **b** what Sir Henry thought of the villagers?

2 From the evidence of sources 3 and 4, do you think Sir Henry's house was built early or late in the sixteenth century?

3 What can you learn from sources 3 and 5 about the lives of sixteenth- and seventeenth-century gentlemen and their families?

SOURCE 5

A banquet at Sir Henry Unton's house in about 1596. This is part of a larger picture which his wife had painted as a memorial when Sir Henry died. Find:
- the guests
- the servants
- the musicians
- the actors.

Citizens and burgesses

Some towns were given a special charter by the Crown which allowed them to elect representatives to the House of Commons. In those towns, known as boroughs, citizens were called burgesses.

William Harrison based his ideas of social rank on how much land people owned. He found it difficult to fit in townspeople (source 6) because they did not own land. He ended up putting wealthy townspeople into a rank of their own and all other townspeople into the 'fourth sort'. In fact, by Elizabeth's reign, many wealthy merchants thought of themselves as gentlemen, while townspeople who owned their own workshops and were doing well, such as better-off bakers and butchers, often described themselves as yeomen.

SOURCE 6

activity

1 What can you tell about sixteenth-century town life from source 6?

2 How do sources 7 and 8 suggest that yeomen became more prosperous in the sixteenth century?

A fête at Bermondsey, near London, painted about 1570, showing townspeople of all ranks.

Yeomen

SOURCE 7

A yeoman's house from Montgomeryshire, Wales. It walls consist of a wooden frame filled in with hazel twigs woven together and covered first in clay and then plaster. It has a straw roof and a floor of beaten earth. It was originally built in the 16th century and then improved in the 17th century when the chimney and the windows were put in. They have sliding panels, but no glass.

Yeomen became more prosperous in the sixteenth century and often built bigger and better houses with several rooms (source 7). According to Harrison:

SOURCE 8

Many farmers . . . have . . . learned . . . to garnish [decorate] their cupboards with plate, their joint-beds with tapestry and silk hangings.

William Harrison, *The Description of England*, 1577

The fourth sort

A husbandman ran his own farm, but farmed much less land than most yeomen. He might just manage to feed his family in a good year; in a bad year they would be in trouble.

Labourers worked for wages and depended on them for their living. They usually lived in cottages with small gardens where the family could grow a few vegetables and maybe keep an animal. Between a quarter and a third of the population were in this group.

Craftspeople living in villages usually farmed a bit of land as well as working at their craft. In towns, they usually sold directly from their workshops. Some could be as well-off as a yeoman, but many, like the village labourers, were very poor.

SOURCE 9

A seventeenth-century woodcut of a woman working in the fields.

Women

SOURCE 10

The Saltonstall family, painted about 1637. Sir Richard Saltonstall leads his son and daughter in, to see their mother and the newly-born baby.

A woman's rank in society depended on the rank of her father or husband. Women had fewer rights than men. They could not vote, even if they owned enough land. They could not be Justices of the Peace, though some did serve as churchwardens. A few townswomen did trade in their own right.

Until she was married, a woman was supposed to obey her parents. Once she was married she was supposed to obey her husband. The father was the head of each family. In the eyes of the law, married women had no rights:

SOURCE 11

Women . . . so soon as they are married are wholly at the will and disposition [disposal] of the husband . . . They can own no goods, not even their clothes.

Edward Chamberlayne, second half of the seventeenth century

A wife's duty was to obey her husband, but one London priest wrote that a wife should also be:

SOURCE 12

The neerest to equality that may be . . . a place [position] . . . wherein man and wife are . . . even fellowes, and partners.

William Gouge, *Of Domesticall Duties: Eight Treatises*, 1622

That is how things often worked out. One man's will said:

SOURCE 13

That what estate [wealth] he had, he together with his wife Jane had got it by their industry [work] and therefore he gave and bequeathed all . . . to be at her disposal, and that if it were more [she] deserved it well.

Will of Edward Newby, 1659

By law, if a married woman became a widow, she was allowed to do what she liked with her property.

SOURCE 14

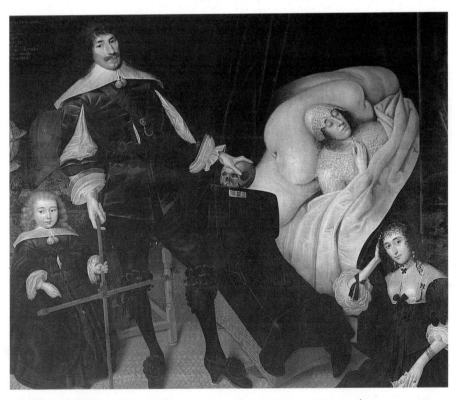

Sir Thomas Aston at the deathbed of his wife in 1635. Sir Thomas was a wealthy gentleman of Cheshire. His wife, Magdalene, is shown twice – as dead (in the bed) and as she appeared when she was alive (at the foot of the bed). Beside Sir Thomas is their son, the only survivor of four children, who died in 1637. Married women often gave birth as many as seven times, but many babies and children died. Also, many adults died between the ages of thirty and forty, and it was unusual for both parents to be alive when a child reached adulthood.

activity

1a What can you learn from (i) sources 3, 5, 6, 9, 10 and 14, (ii) sources 11–13 about the lives of women?
b Are (i) the pictures, (ii) the written sources most useful? Explain your reasons.

Why did some people get richer and some get poorer?

Between 1500 and 1650 some people became very much richer and some very much poorer. On the whole, those who owned a lot of land, such as gentlemen and yeomen, were the ones who got richer, and those with smaller amounts of land, such as husbandmen, or none at all, such as labourers, got poorer. Not only that, but the number of poor people increased. Here are some of the reasons.

Prices

SOURCE 15

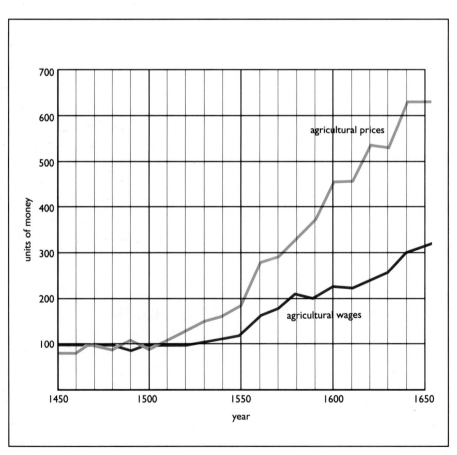

Agricultural prices and wages, 1450–1650. The graph shows wages in 1450 as being equal to 100 units of money.

SOURCE 16

The changing value of wages 1450–1750. This graph allows you to compare the amounts of food labourers' wages would buy in different years. It is based on taking the years 1451–75 as ones in which labourers' wages would buy 100 units of food. There are gaps in those years for which information is not available.

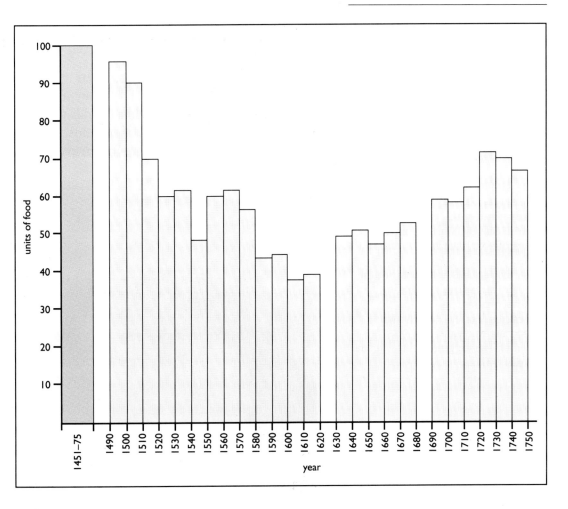

SOURCE 17

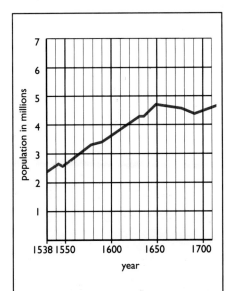

Population 1538–1700. In 1538 Thomas Cromwell, Henry VIII's minister, ordered every parish to keep a register of baptisms, marriages and burials. Historians use these registers to estimate the size of the population.

Prices rose nearly seven times between 1500 and 1650, but peoples' wages did not rise as fast and keep up with them (source 15). The price rise was good news for farmers, such as gentlemen and yeomen, who had enough land to feed their families and to produce a surplus to sell. They made large profits.

It was bad news for cottagers, labourers and craftspeople who had very little land of their own and had to buy their food in the market. Because their wages did not go up too, they could afford to buy less food (source 16). Their lives became even harder.

Population

Between 1538 and 1650 the population grew very fast (source 17). This meant there were more children to feed in each household, which was difficult for poorer families. It also meant there were more people needing land. The oldest son inherited his parents' land; but the younger sons and their families had to find new land for themselves. Many of them left their villages to find land elsewhere or to go to a town, often London, where they hoped to find work.

> **i Enclosed**   *An enclosed field is one with hedges or fences round it.*

Farming for profit

As the price of food went up, yeomen wanted more land in order to make bigger profits (source 18). They also found it was more efficient to farm several **enclosed** fields rather than to have many strips scattered throughout open fields. So they used some of their profit to buy up the neighbouring strips belonging to husbandmen.

SOURCE 18

A late seventeenth-century farm house in Surrey. Many yeomen used their profits to have large houses built.
Find:
● the arch shapes above the bottom windows and in the chimney
● the two-storey porch
● the lines of brick-work which decorate the walls
How do these suggest that the farmer was well off?

SOURCE 19

A room in a seventeenth-century farm house. The table is laid for supper.
Find:
● wooden beakers
● pewter bowls. Pewter is a mixture of tin and lead
● spoons. Few people used forks until the end of the seventeenth century.
How do the objects in the room suggest that the family living here was fairly prosperous?

Meanwhile, many gentlemen realised their land was worth more so they put up the rent. Husbandmen had only enough land to feed their families in the first place. They had no surplus and made no profits, so they could not afford higher rents. John Wilson was typical of many who made special requests, or petitions, to their landlords not to raise the rent:

SOURCE 20

Otherwise your poor petitioner, his wife, and eight poor children . . . knows no other way out but . . . to give over [up] your honour's land, by reason of the dear renting thereof, and so be constrained [forced] to go a-begging up and down the countrie.

Petition of John Wilson to the Earl of Northumberland, late 17th century

Enclosure of common land

Husbandmen who decided to sell up or to leave their land became labourers and then depended on wages for their living. Rising prices were already bad for labourers. Their position was made worse because the gentry and yeomen also found extra land by creating and enclosing fields on what was supposed to be common land.

Labourers depended on this common land to survive. It was the equivalent of extra pay. They used it to graze their few animals, as a source of wood for houses and fuel, as a source of braken for bedding and as a place to trap rabbits and birds for food. The loss of these rights helped to cause some people to take to the road to try to find more labouring work elsewhere and others to look for work, such as weaving, which some of the family could do at home.

activity

1 Look at sources 15–20 and the information in the text. Here are four changes that happened between 1500 and 1650:
a the price rise;
b the population rise;
c farming for profit;
d enclosures.
Who do you think (i) gained, (ii) lost from each change? Explain your reasons.

How the government dealt with the poor

SOURCE 21

This engraving of 1659 shows the rich man and the poor man.

The problem

Throughout the sixteenth century, governments became increasingly worried about the poor. In particular they were alarmed by the number of beggars who wandered from place to place and who were known as 'vagrants' or 'vagabonds'.

Some of these vagabonds were soldiers discharged from the army, some were sailors who had returned from a voyage, some were poor people or monks who had lived in monasteries until Henry VIII closed them. Many others were those forced to leave home because of changes in prices, population and farming methods (see pages 58–61).

The solution

It had always been the custom to give alms, or charitable gifts, to those known as the 'impotent [powerless] poor', who were unable to earn their living because they were too young, too old, too ill or disabled. These people were also thought of as 'deserving poor'. A shepherd from Foxton in Cambridgeshire, who was certainly not wealthy himself, left in his will:

SOURCE 22

To William Symton, John Gibson, William Baker, Joan Skynner, Elyn Godfrey, John Richardson and to Dionyse Curteyse my poore nighbours to each of them 3d.

Will of David Alanson, 1524

In the middle of the sixteenth century, the impotent poor relied on individual acts of charity of this kind. But the government took a very tough line with able-bodied beggars and vagabonds. The first time they were caught they were whipped; the second time they were whipped again and had the upper part of their right ear cut off; the third time they were hanged.

activity

I Work in small groups.
Look at source 24.
a Discuss why William
Sturmyn might have decided
to release the vagrant.
b Devise and act out a scene
in which William (i) comes
across the vagrant, (ii)
decides to release him, (iii)
does so.
c Decide (i) how, (ii) when,
(iii) where you think
William's parents found out
what he had done.
d Devise and act out a scene
in which William's parents
find out, showing what they
and he feel about what he
has done.
e Put your two scenes
together and show them to
the class.
f Discuss which scenes were
(i) most, (ii) least likely.

activity

2 Here are three types of
poor people to be found in
sixteenth and seventeenth
centuries:
a able-bodied people who
did not want to work;
b very young, old, ill or
disabled people;
c able-bodied people who
wanted to work, but could
find none.
Use the information in the
text to decide which of these
groups the government
thought was the most
deserving of support and
which was the least
deserving. Explain your
answers.

SOURCE 23

Whipping through the streets.

However, some people may have had sympathy for vagrants,
such as this boy from Foxton:

SOURCE 24

*1542. They say that William Sturmyn junior set free a certain
begging vagrant taken by the constable and lawfully placed and kept in
the stocks . . . and without authority freed the said vagabond . . . and
allowed him to escape unlawfully. So William is fined 6s 8d.*

Quoted in R. Parker, *The Common Stream*, 1976

As the number of poor increased, towns such as London and
Norwich found themselves full of vagrants. They started to set up
schemes to deal with the problem locally and later the government
used some of their ideas to set up a national system. The national
system was completed in 1601 and was supervised in each shire by
the Justices of the Peace.

There were two big changes from the way things had been before.
Firstly, the system recognised that many able bodied poor people
wanted work, but could not find it. They were now to be given
materials to make things in their homes and paid for what they
made.

Secondly, the better-off people in each parish were to pay a
compulsory tax, called the Poor Rate. JPs had to appoint two or
more Overseers of the Poor in each parish to collect the Poor Rate
and then give money from it to the impotent poor.

The death penalty for vagrants was ended. But one thing stayed
the same: vagrants who were caught were to be whipped and sent
to work in a House of Correction.

This system of poor relief stayed more or less unchanged until
1834.

Different regions

SOURCE 25

Farming regions in England and Wales 1500–1640.

Wood pasture

This system was used in lowland areas where there were woods and forests as well as pasture. People here lived in small farms, usually separate from one another. They grew some crops but mainly went in for dairy and cattle farming. They usually combined this with work such as weaving, mining and metal working.

Open pasture

This system was used in highland areas of mountain and moor where there was plenty of grass, but the soil was not good enough to grow many crops. People lived mainly by rearing cattle and sheep, and growing a few crops on a fenced 'in-field' which was used for several years without lying fallow. Then it was abandoned and another area fenced in. People lived in farms and hamlets, often far apart, and shared the common pastures.

0   50   100km

PENNINES

York

PEAK DISTRICT

FENS

CAMBRIAN MOUNTAINS

FOREST OF ARDEN

COTSWOLDS

SALISBURY PLAIN

London

NORTH DOWNS

THE WEALD

SOUTH DOWNS

Exeter

KEY

mixed farming

open pasture

wood pasture

activity

I Look at source 25.
a What was the main farming system in (i) Wales, (ii) the north and west of England, (iii) the south and east of England?
b Mixed farming produced the most corn. Which were the chief corn-producing areas of England and Wales?

Mixed farming

This was the system used mainly in lowland areas of central England. 'Open', or unhedged, fields (usually three or four) were divided into strips. These were divided among tenants to give everyone a balance of good and bad land for growing crops. One field in turn lay **fallow** each year and was used for animals to graze. Everyone had the right to use meadows and wasteland. People lived in villages and had to co-operate to organise their work.

i Fallow   A field that lay fallow was left unused for a year so that the goodness could return to its soil. The grazing animals also helped to fertilise it with their dung.

activity

2 Use source 25 and the information in the text to say what effects you think the price rise might have had on areas of (i) mixed farming, (ii) wood pasture, (iii) open pasture. Explain your reasons.

Most families lived and worked in the countryside and made their living from farming. But it would be wrong to think of all farms and villages as the same. There were different types of farming in various parts of the country (source 25). Each type created its own way of life for people.

The change to farming for profit took place especially in the mixed farming areas that produced the most corn. Many of the people who decided to leave their home went to the parts of the country with open pasture and wood pasture where it was easier to find land and start again.

assignments

1 Use the information and sources in Parts 2, 4 and 5 to make a display using words, pictures, maps and diagrams to illustrate the lives of people in different ranks of society in the sixteenth century.

2a Change can be good for some people and bad for others. Make a list of those groups who (i) gained, (ii) lost from the rise in prices between 1500 and 1650.
b Write a paragraph to explain how each group gained or lost.

3 Between 1500 and 1650 the number of poor people increased.
a Use sources 15–25 and the information in the text to make lists of (i) some of the causes of this change, (ii) some of its consequences.
b Which (i) cause, (ii) consequence do you think was the most important?
c Explain how (i) the price rise, (ii) the population growth helped to cause an increase in the number of poor people.
d Explain how these two causes were linked to each other.

4 Use the sources and information on pages 62–63.
a Make a chart to show what (i) changed, (ii) stayed the same in the way the government treated poor people in the sixteenth century.
b Do you think the way the government treated vagabonds after 1601 was an improvement on the way it had treated them in the mid-sixteenth century? Give your reasons.

5a In Part 5 find an example of each of the following types of source: (i) a painting, (ii) a will, (iii) a petition, (iv) a court judgement, (v) a pamphlet or book.
b Explain how each one is useful in telling us about the lives of ordinary people.
c Which ones do you think are (i) the least useful, (ii) the most useful? Give reasons for your answers.

6
Civil War

'All the birds are flown'

On 3 January 1642 King Charles I accused five members of the House of Commons and one member of the House of Lords of High Treason. He said they were trying to take away his rightful powers as king and he ordered Parliament to hand them over to him. Parliament did nothing.

At about three o'clock the following afternoon a messenger arrived at Westminster to speak to John Pym, the leader of the five members in the Commons. The messenger said that the King himself was on his way from Whitehall Palace with a party of guards and would be arriving shortly to arrest the five members. Pym immediately informed the Commons and asked the Speaker to allow him and the other four to leave. They went out to the riverside, where a barge was waiting, and were on their way down the Thames to the City of London when the King reached Westminster.

The King left his guards in the lobby of the House of Commons, with the door open so that the members could see them. As Charles went in, he took off his hat as a mark of respect. The members stood up, taking off their hats too.

The King looked at the place where Pym usually sat and, not seeing him there, walked towards the Speaker's chair. 'By your leave, Mr Speaker,' he said, 'I must borrow your chair a little.' The

SOURCE 1

An engraving showing Charles I entering the Commons on 4 January 1642 to arrest the five members.

activity

I The information in the text about the King entering the Commons is based on sources written by people who were there at the time.

a How do source I and the information based on the written sources (i) disagree, (ii) agree about what happened?

b Do you think the artist who engraved source I was there at the time?

activity

2 How does source 3 suggest that the Commons had become more independent of the Crown since Elizabeth I's time? The information on pages 19–21 will help you to answer.

ⓘ Anthony Van Dyck *Sir Anthony Van Dyck (1599–1641) was a Flemish artist, born in Antwerp, Belgium. Charles I invited him to England in 1632. He was Court painter until his death. His way of painting portraits influenced artists for the next hundred years.*

Speaker made way for him and Charles stood by the chair scanning the faces of the silent members. Then he told them why he had come and finished by saying:

SOURCE 2

> *Since I see all the birds are flown, I do expect from you that you shall send them unto me as soon as they return hither [here].*
>
> John Rushworth, *Historical Collections*, 1659

Then the King asked the Speaker if he could see any of the five. The Speaker, falling on his knees, reminded the King that he was the servant of the Commons, not of the Crown:

SOURCE 3

> *May it please your Majesty, I have neither eyes to see nor tongue to speak in this place, but as the House is pleased to direct me.*
>
> John Rushworth, *Historical Collections*, 1659

As Charles walked out of the House, the Commons broke into uproar.

SOURCE 4

Charles I in 1633, a detail from a painting by **Anthony Van Dyck**.

Why could the King and Parliament not agree?

Charles I's relationship with Parliament had become so bad that the Lords and Commons protected people whom he called traitors, while he took the risk of appearing to be a bully and a tyrant by turning up at Westminster with armed men. Why had their relationship become so bad? Why couldn't they agree?

Parliament's grievances

Charles became king in 1625 when his father, James I and VI, died. The Crown was short of money because of the rise in prices and wars against France and Spain, and so Charles needed to ask Parliament for taxes. The Commons often criticised him and offered advice he did not want to take.

In 1629 he made peace with France and Spain and decided to see if he could make do without calling Parliament. He managed for eleven years. In some ways he ruled well; but when Parliament next met in 1640 the first things the Commons wanted to discuss were their 'grievances', or complaints. The two biggest concerned taxation and religion.

Taxation

Even without a war, the Crown needed extra money. In 1635 Charles ordered the whole country to pay a tax called Ship Money (source 5). The Crown did not need Parliament's agreement to collect this particular tax and, in the past, it had asked only coastal towns to pay it.

Country gentlemen, who hated paying taxes anyway, realised the King had found a clever way to raise more money without having to call Parliament.

SOURCE 5

The 'Great Charles', built in 1637 with the proceeds of Ship Money. The tax was used to pay for improvements to the navy which most people agreed were needed. This engraving was made to try to persuade people that Charles I was right to ask more people to pay Ship Money. The ship was later re-named the 'Sovereign of the Seas'.

Religion

By Charles I's time, very many country gentlemen were Puritans and so were their parish priests, or ministers. They thought it was important to read and discuss the Bible, and to listen to sermons. They had very little ceremony in their church services because it reminded them of the Catholic Church. The ministers did not wear special robes.

Charles I was the first monarch to be brought up as a member of the Church of England. He loved its services and ceremonies. He thought of it as the true Church and he expected his subjects to follow its beliefs and services exactly.

He supported the Archbishop of Canterbury, William Laud, who wanted priests to make church services more holy. He insisted they wore the correct robes and followed the exact words of the Prayer Book. He told them to move communion tables from the middle of the church, where they had stood since Elizabeth I's time, and put them at the east end. They were to put rails round them, call them altars, and bow to them.

The Puritans suspected the King and Laud of wanting to restore the Catholic Church. Their fears were all the greater because Charles's French wife, Henrietta Maria, was a Catholic and was allowed to have her own Catholic priest at Court.

The king's mistake

Crown and Parliament obviously could not quarrel when Parliament was not sitting. So long as Charles did not need to fight a war, he could manage without Parliament. His mistake was to provoke a war with his own subjects in Scotland.

Charles was the first monarch to inherit the three crowns of England, Ireland and Scotland. He never visited Ireland and, unlike James VI and I, he did not have a close feeling for the way people thought and felt in Scotland, even though he was born there.

The Scottish Kirk was Presbyterian and had always used different church services from those in England. Charles wanted all his subjects to worship in the same way. In 1637 he ordered the Scots to use a new Prayer Book like the one used in England. The first time it was used in St Giles Cathedral in Edinburgh, the congregation rioted and hurled wooden stools and sticks at the priests.

Scots everywhere signed a National Covenant, or promise, swearing to defend their Kirk. Charles saw this as rebellion. He raised an army from the English militia, marched north, and then realised that those who had signed the Covenant, the Covenanters, were too strong for him. In 1640 he had to call Parliament to ask for money to recruit a properly-paid army.

The Commons refused to grant the money unless the King listened to their grievances first. Furious, Charles dismissed the

SOURCE 6

The Arch-Prelate of St Andrewes in Scotland reading the new Service-booke in his pontificalibus assaulted by men & Women, with Cricketts stooles Stickes and Stones.

There were riots like this against the Prayer Book throughout Scotland in 1637. Charles and Laud discussed the Prayer Book with the Scottish bishops, but the King consulted neither the Scottish Parliament, nor the General Assembly of the Kirk.

Parliament. The Scottish army then crossed the border into England and defeated Charles's troops. The King agreed to pay the Scottish army's expenses while he negotiated with them. He did not have the money, so he had to call another Parliament.

Parliament's victory

This time Charles had to agree to whatever Parliament demanded. Within a year the Lords and Commons had abolished all the powers the King had used during his years of personal rule. He agreed not to use any of his unpopular money-raising methods again, including Ship Money. He agreed to abandon Laud's rules for the Church and its services. He even agreed to a law which said that Parliament must meet every three years. The Crown would never again be able to rule for long without Parliament. The King had given in; Parliament had won.

activity

I How does the information in the text show that Charles I:
a wanted to get rid of the differences in the way his subjects followed their religion;
b was out of touch with the attitudes and opinions of many of his subjects?

SOURCE 7

John Pym painted by **Samuel Cooper**.

> **i** **Samuel Cooper**   Samuel
> Cooper (1609–1672)
> was a musician (he played the
> lute), linguist and poet, as well
> as an artist. He specialised in
> painting very small portraits
> called 'miniatures'.

activity

2 Imagine you are an adviser
to Charles I. What advice
would you give him **a** in
favour of, **b** against
attempting to arrest the five
members? Explain your
reasons.
3 Write the speech you
think John Pym might have
given in the House of
Commons to get members
to support his plan to
remove control of the militia
from the Crown and give it
to Parliament instead.

The collapse of trust

When one side in a quarrel gives in and agrees with the other, it usually means the matter is settled and the quarrel ends. But this is not always the case. Suppose the person who has won thinks the one who has given in is only pretending to agree and will try to find a way to start up the quarrel again. Suppose they are right, and the one who has given in really is looking for a way to win in the end. That is what happened in 1641.

Even though the King agreed to Parliament's demands, John Pym (source 7) and his friends in the Lords and Commons did not believe he meant to keep to the agreement. Meanwhile, Charles was looking for a way to restore his powers, by force if necessary.

Events in Charles's third kingdom, Ireland, brought matters to a crisis. In October 1641 the Irish Catholics rebelled, fearing that the puritan English Parliament was about to pass more laws against Catholics. About 3,000 Protestants were killed in Ulster, one in five of the population.

The King needed an army to put down the rebellion, but Pym feared he would use it against his opponents in Parliament. He did not trust Charles. He said that the King was secretly in league with the Irish Catholics. He demanded that Parliament, not the Crown, should have control of the militia.

Pym was now trying to take away one of the Crown's oldest rights. Charles was in a corner. He had to get rid of Pym. One thing encouraged him – members of Parliament were starting to feel that Pym had gone too far. He and his puritan friends were even suggesting that Parliament should abolish bishops and the Prayer Book. Charles had some supporters in Parliament at last. In January 1642 he decided to accuse his chief opponents of High Treason.

The King's gamble

As Charles led his guards out of Whitehall Palace to arrest the five members, he was taking a huge gamble. If he succeeded, those who opposed him would lose their leaders and the opposition would collapse. If he failed, Pym would be able to claim that the King was prepared to use force against his own Parliament. Charles would be unable to put the blame onto someone else because he was leading the guards himself.

Charles did fail. Pym was too clever for him and the five members escaped. The people of London sided with them and that night barricades went up in the city. It was too dangerous for Charles and the Court to stay. Within a week they left for Windsor.

The war begins

Cavalier came from the Spanish word 'cavaliero' which in turn came from 'caballero' which meant a trooper on horse-back. To the English in 1641 it meant a brutal Catholic-Spanish trooper, and enemy of Protestants – the perfect insult for Parliamentarians to throw at Royalists. Later the word came to mean a gallant and free-and-easy courtier or gentleman.

Roundhead was the nickname originally given to the apprentices of London because they had their hair cut very short to give themselves a bullet-headed look. In 1641 Pym used the apprentices to riot outside the Parliament House and frighten members into supporting his proposals. The Royalists started to call Pym and all his supporters 'Roundheads' to show that they despised them. Pym himself, like most Parliamentarians, wore his hair long in the fashion of the time (see source 7).

Royalists and Parliamentarians

Nobody wanted a civil war in 1642. It happened because a few members of the population – those in Parliament – failed to agree and split into two sides. The King, most of the Lords and some of the Commons were on one side. Most of the Commons and some of the Lords were on the other. Those on the King's side were known as Royalists and those on the other as Parliamentarians. They nicknamed each other **Cavaliers** and **Roundheads**.

The King raised the royal standard outside Nottingham in August 1642 as a signal that he was collecting an army. He sent messages to the Lord Lieutenant of every shire ordering people to support him. Parliament sent messages ordering everyone to disobey. In this way the rest of the country became involved in the quarrel. How did people decide which side to take and who to obey?

Taking sides

One thing – religion – divided people more than anything else. People who sympathised with the kind of Church the Puritans wanted always supported Parliament. Those who preferred the kind of Church Laud had tried to create supported the King.

Most ordinary people did their best to keep out of the war altogether. If an army came their way, they did as they were told until it went away again. Some became more involved because they had to support whichever side their landlord chose.

Some landowning gentlemen tried to keep out of the war too; but many were drawn in. Some supported the side they thought would win. Others thought carefully about what each side stood for. The war divided people who were normally close. It split up families and it separated friends.

The Verney family was split by the war. Sir Edmund decided to support the King. His son, Sir Ralph, declared for Parliament. Sir Edmund told a friend:

SOURCE 8

For my part I do not like the quarrel, and do heartily wish that the King would consent to what they desire . . . I have served him for thirty years, and will not do so base [treacherous] a thing as to desert him . . . I have no liking for Bishops, for whom this quarrel is being fought.

Clarendon, *Memoirs*, written mid-seventeenth century

activity

I Look at source 8.
a How does it suggest that Sir Edmund Verney sympathised with the Parliamentarians?
b Why did he side with the King?

activity

2 Look at source 9.
a Do you think Lady Sussex was a Royalist or a Parliamentarian?
b Why do you think she begs Sir Ralph to 'give nothing to Parliament'?
3 Look at source 10.
a Why do you think Waller calls the Civil War 'this war without an enemy'?
b How does his letter suggest (i) he is unhappy to be fighting the war, (ii) he believes in what he is doing?

On his way to the first battle of the war (in which he was killed) Sir Edmund wrote to another friend, Lady Sussex, and she then wrote to Sir Ralph:

SOURCE 9

Your father's letter was a sad one, and he said this of you, 'Madam, he has ever been near my heart and truly is there still' . . . he is much troubled you declare yourself for Parliament . . . For God's sake give nothing to Parliament . . . I hope in the Lord there will be peace and that Parliament will show their strength and so cause the King to yield [give in] to most of their demands.

Lady Sussex, Letter to Sir Ralph Verney, 1642

Before the war, Sir Ralph Hopton and Sir William Waller were close friends. They chose opposite sides and became generals commanding rival armies in the west of England. Before their first battle they exchanged letters. Waller said the war could not alter his feelings of friendship for Hopton. He went on to say:

SOURCE 10

God . . . knows with what a sad heart I go upon this service, and with what a perfect hatred I detest this war without an enemy . . . but . . . we are both set upon a stage and must both act those parts given us in this tragedy: Let us do it with honour and without personal dislike.

Sir William Waller, Letter to Sir Ralph Hopton, 16 June, 1643

A few weeks later he defeated his friend in a battle at Lansdown near Bath.

SOURCE 11

Sir Ralph Hopton (1598–1652), painted by an unknown artist in about 1637. Sir Ralph became a Royalist general.

'A lone woman'

Women fought in the war as well as men. Lady Bankes and her maids, whose names we do not know, defended Corfe Castle against a Parliamentary siege. The women of Lyme Regis helped to defend their town against the Royalists.

Women also tried to stop the war. In Bristol they opened the gates to prevent citizens from defending the town against an approaching force. In Derby they tried to stop people paying taxes for the war.

Susan Rodway's husband fought for Parliament with one of the London trained bands. This letter shows she was one of the many women and men who simply wanted a normal life:

SOURCE 12

Most dear and loving husband, my king love. I remember me unto you, hoping that you are in good health, as I am ... I pray you to come home, if you can come safely ... I do desire to hear from you as soon as you can ... You do not consider I am a lone woman; I thought you would never leave me thus long ... so I rest ever praying for your safest return. Your loving wife, Susan Rodway.

From Mercurius Aulicus, 1643

activity

I How does source 12 suggest that:
a Susan Rodway did not expect her husband to be away for so long;
b the rights and wrongs of the Civil War probably did not matter to many people?

Why did Parliament win the war?

Nobody expected the Civil War to last very long. Most thought it would be decided by the first battle. They were wrong. The first battle at Edgehill (source 13a) was indecisive and the war went on until 1646. Then Charles I gave himself up to the Scottish army which had joined Parliament against him two years before.

The King started out with several advantages. He was supported by some very wealthy men, so he had money. He had one simple aim, which was to capture London – that would immediately end what he saw as the rebellion. Finally, he was the King. Many on the parliamentary side did not like fighting their own king; they would certainly not have killed him in battle; and they hoped not to have to defeat him too heavily. Their aims were, at first, not so simple as the King's. They wanted to force him to negotiate.

So why, in the end, did the King lose and Parliament win?

SOURCE 13a

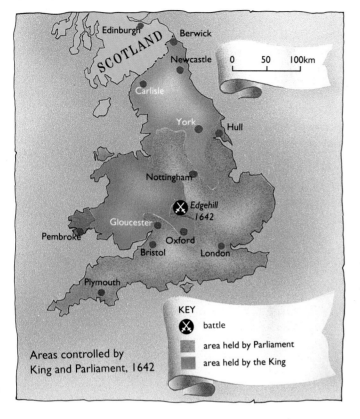

Areas controlled by
King and Parliament, 1642

KEY
⊗ battle
area held by Parliament
area held by the King

SOURCE 13b

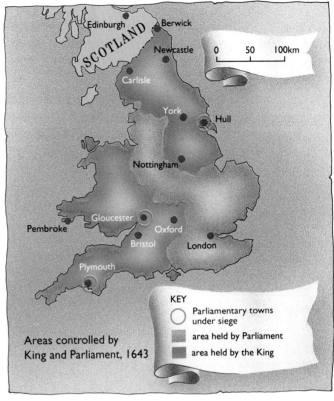

Areas controlled by
King and Parliament, 1643

KEY
◯ Parliamentary towns under siege
area held by Parliament
area held by the King

SOURCE 13c

Areas controlled by
King and Parliament, 1644

KEY
⊗ battle
area held by Parliament
area held by the King

SOURCE 13d

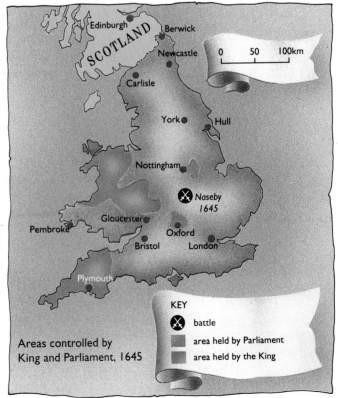

Areas controlled by
King and Parliament, 1645

KEY
⊗ battle
area held by Parliament
area held by the King

Areas controlled by the King and Parliament, 1642–45.

The Scots

Both sides looked for allies once they realised the war would not be short. Charles managed to make peace with the Irish Catholics, which allowed his army in Ireland to return home to help him in England.

Parliament did better. In 1643 Pym agreed with the Scots that if Parliament won the war, it would set up a Presbyterian Church in England like the one in Scotland. In return, an army of 20,000 Scots invaded England as an ally of Parliament. In July 1644 the Scottish and parliamentary armies combined to beat the Royalists at Marston Moor (source 13c) and so won control of the north of England.

New officers

In 1645 Parliament made a rule called the Self-Denying Ordinance (order). It said that no member of the Lords or Commons could go on being an army officer. That meant that two parliamentary generals, the Earls of Essex and Manchester, had to resign. Parliament made an exception. It said that Colonel Oliver Cromwell could remain a member of the Commons and carry on being a cavalry officer.

The new rule was a clever way to get rid of Manchester and Essex. Cromwell and others suspected them of not wishing to defeat the King in battle. Manchester was Cromwell's commanding officer. One day he told Cromwell:

SOURCE 14

If we beat the King ninety and nine times, yet he is king still . . . but if the King beat us once we shall all be hanged . . .

Quoted in C. Russell, *The Crisis of Parliaments 1509–1660*, 1971

Cromwell replied:

SOURCE 15

My lord, if this be so, why did we ever take up arms at first?

Quoted in C. Russell, *The Crisis of Parliaments 1509–1660*, 1971

Parliament then appointed a new general, Sir Thomas Fairfax, commander of the Northern army that had won at Marston Moor. Unlike most commanders Fairfax had been a soldier before the Civil War. Everyone on the parliamentary side respected him. Cromwell became Lieutenant-General in charge of the cavalry.

The New Model Army

The army Fairfax commanded was a new one, made up of
Parliament's three existing armies, two of which had been formed to
defend their own regions – East Anglia and the south of England.
Parliament now needed one large army that would go anywhere
and attack royalist territory. It had to be led well, drilled well and
paid well – in other words, professional. Because of this, Parliament
called it the 'New Model Army'. Royalists called it the 'New Noddle',
but, all the same, it beat them at Naseby in June 1645 (sources 13d
and 16). Naseby was the last major battle of the war.

SOURCE 16

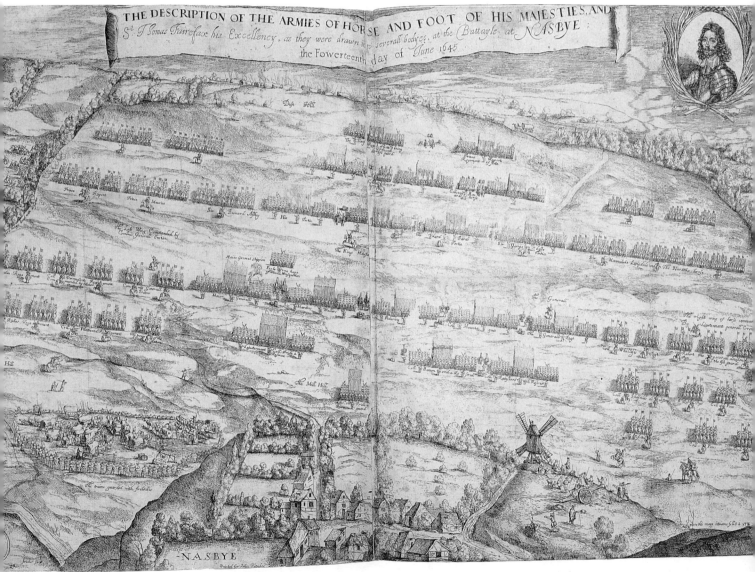

The battle of Naseby. The King's army is at the top of the picture. Find:
- the village of Naseby
- the villagers watching
- the royalist and parliamentarian baggage trains
- artillery, cavalry and infantry. Infantry carried either muskets or pikes.

Money

Parliament was in a better position than the King to find money for a long war. The King had rich supporters, but they ran out of money themselves. Both sides taxed people in their areas very heavily, but the Parliamentarians were better at collecting taxes than the Royalists. They also controlled London with its rich merchants.

The most important thing about the New Model Army was that it was well-paid. This meant that soldiers were willing to serve in it and to drill and train. In the end, the King ran out of money. His soldiers at Naseby were badly equipped compared to those of Parliament. After Naseby he might have recruited another army; but he had no money to pay the soldiers.

The unpopularity of the war

By 1645 people were fed up with the war and they wanted it to end. They were tired of the arguments (source 17) and the bloodshed, tired of paying heavy taxes, tired of being made to give food and shelter to troops, and tired of seeing crops destroyed and buildings looted (source 18). In some places, groups were formed to try to keep soldiers of both sides out of an area, but they did not have much success.

SOURCE 17

Reading the newspaper outside a shoemaker's shop in Norwich. Both sides published newspapers giving the news about the war from their own point of view.

activity

I Use the sources and information on pages 74–79 to make lists of **a** the strengths, **b** the weaknesses of (i) the King, (ii) Parliament in the Civil War.

SOURCE 18

An engraving which shows parliamentary puritan soldiers removing altar rails and the cross from a church.

The Souldiers in their passage to York turn unto reformers pull down Popish pictures, break down rayles, turn altars into Tables

The reason why the King had no money to pay for a new army after Naseby, was that most gentlemen in the areas he controlled refused to give him any – and he no longer had enough soldiers left to make them pay.

assignments

1 Look at source 10 and the information in the text. Before Waller wrote this letter, Hopton suggested a meeting between them. The meeting never took place. It is possible that Hopton hoped to persuade Waller to change sides. Imagine the meeting between them did in fact take place. Use the sources and information in Part 6 to write:
a what you think Hopton might have said to Waller to persuade him to change sides;
b what you think Waller might have said in reply?
You could, if you wish, set it out as a discussion between them in the form of a play.

2 Use the sources and information on pages 74–79.
a Make a list of reasons why you think Parliament won the Civil War. Write a few sentences about each one.
b Choose what you think were the two most important and the two least important reasons. Explain your choices.
c What were the links between (i) money, (ii) military success, and (iii) popular opinion in causing the victory of Parliament and the defeat of the King?
d Which of these do you think was the most important? Explain your reasons.

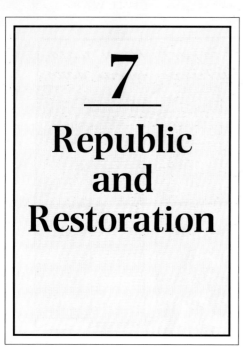

7
Republic and Restoration

The trial and execution of Charles I

SOURCE 1

The trial of Charles I. Find:
- the judges
- clerks at a table taking notes
- the King, sitting alone, facing them
- the lawyers next to the King
- the spectators. Special galleries were built for them
- guards armed with spears or muskets.

On 20 January 1649, a special court set up by Parliament met in Westminster Hall to try Charles I (source 1). He was accused of trying to rule in a tyrannical way and of causing all the bloodshed and misery that occurred in the Civil War.

Parliament appointed 135 people to act as judges, but only about 85 turned up. The rest were frightened or disagreed with what they were being asked to do. Everyone knew that it was unheard of to try a king. The President of the court, John Bradshaw, wore a hat with a metal lining (source 2) in case someone tried to shoot him.

Charles was usually a shy man who stammered. In the court his stammer left him and he spoke clearly and confidently. He refused to answer the charges against him. He said no court could try a king because all proper courts were the King's courts. He said this was not a proper court anyway. It had power, he said, in the same way that a robber with a pistol had power. What would happen to justice if anyone could set up a court, just because they happened to have power?

The judges sentenced the King to death, as he knew they would. The day of the execution was icy cold. Charles put on an extra shirt so that he would not shiver on the scaffold and appear to be afraid. He was taken to the royal palace at Whitehall and then through a window in the Banqueting House to the scaffold outside (source 3). It was hung with black and surrounded by troopers on horseback to keep back the crowds.

Charles made a short speech to those with him on the scaffold. Then he took off his jewels and outer clothes and put his hair under a cap to keep it clear of the axe. He knelt down, prayed, and then stretched forward his arms as a signal. The axe came down and cut off his head in one blow. A great groan went up from the crowd and the troopers immediately cleared the streets.

SOURCE 2

John Bradshaw's hat.

activity

1 How would you describe Charles I's behaviour at his trial and execution?
2 Why do you think a great groan went up from the crowd when Charles I was executed?

SOURCE 3

The execution of Charles I.

Why was Charles I executed?

Charles had given himself up to the Scots in 1646. Because he refused to give them what they wanted, they handed him over to Parliament which then started to negotiate with him. Although they still had not reached agreement by 1647, there was no question of executing the King. So why was he executed two years later?

The army takes control

Once the war was over, Parliament wanted some soldiers to go home and the rest to go to Ireland to put down the rebellion there. The soldiers were owed many weeks pay and refused to go until they were given it. Fairfax and Cromwell, now a general, supported them. The army no longer trusted Parliament. In 1647 a junior officer captured the King and took him into the army's control. The officers then started their own negotiations with Charles.

The King betrays a trust

Instead of accepting his defeat and negotiating with the officers honestly, Charles tricked them. He secretly negotiated with the Scots as well, offering to set up a Prebyterian Church in England if they would fight a new war on his behalf. The Scots agreed and, supported by royalist uprisings in England, their army crossed the border in 1648 to start the second Civil War.

A new mood in the army

The war was quickly over after Cromwell's defeat of the Scots near Preston (source 4). But the mood in the army had changed. The King had deliberately provoked another war. The officers called him a 'man of blood'. They said he would always stand in the way of peace. An officer called Colonel Pride went to Parliament and sent away all the members who still favoured negotiating with Charles. Those that remained, known as the 'Rump', agreed with the army that the only way forward was to execute the King. Charles was condemned before his trial began.

activity

1a Work in pairs. Most officers, including Oliver Cromwell, were very reluctant to order the trial and execution of the King. Imagine a discussion in which they are trying to decide what to do. What do you think they would say (i) in favour of, (ii) against executing the King?
b Discuss your ideas with other pairs.

Wales, Ireland and Scotland

Royalist resistance

> **i** **Republic**   A state in which the supreme power belongs to the people and those they elect to represent and govern them.

After the execution of Charles I, England became a **republic**, but the Rump Parliament still had to face the fact that in many people's eyes his eldest son, who had remained abroad during the war, was now King Charles II. Wales had been strongly royalist in the Civil War and still was. In Ireland, the Catholic rebels had joined up with a royalist army and Charles might decide to invade England from there. The Scots declared him to be king.

SOURCE 4

The second Civil War, and Cromwell's campaigns in Ireland and Scotland.

SOURCE 5

Oliver Cromwell, an unfinished portrait by Samuel Cooper done some time after 1653 when Cromwell was Lord Protector. Cromwell was a landowner in Huntingdonshire. He entered Parliament in 1628.

Parliament decided that Wales was royalist because very few Welsh people were Puritans. So it set up a 'Committee for the Propagation [increase] of the Gospel in Wales' to put this right. The committee provided Welsh Bibles and Welsh-speaking preachers, got rid of Church of England priests and tried to replace them with puritan ministers. Although this plan was only partly a success, puritan ideas started to become more popular in Wales at this time.

Parliament put Oliver Cromwell (source 5) in charge of an army to go to deal with the Catholics and Royalists in Ireland. Even before it arrived, a parliamentary force defeated the Royalists in battle. Cromwell then besieged and captured a series of towns (source 4) and, after a year, was able to leave General Ireton to finish the work.

When Cromwell returned from Ireland he was made commander-in-chief of the army because Fairfax had resigned. His next task was to deal with the Scots. After failing to persuade them to send away Charles II, who was now in Scotland, he defeated them at Dunbar (source 4) in 1650. The following year at Worcester (source 4), he defeated a combined Scottish and Royalist army. Charles escaped abroad in disguise.

Case study: Cromwell at Drogheda

The massacre

The first siege carried out by Cromwell's army in Ireland was at the town of Drogheda (sources 4 and 6). When his troops finally broke through the walls, they killed nearly all the defenders, and many priests, women and children too. About 3,000 people died.

Historians agree that Cromwell was responsible for this terrible massacre. There are two interpretations of what happened. One leads to a hard judgement on Cromwell, the other to a soft judgement. The soft one says Cromwell should not be totally condemned for what happened because some of his actions can be justified. The hard one says he should be condemned completely.

SOURCE 6

The storming of Drogheda.

Different interpretations: the soft judgement

This interpretation says that Cromwell should be judged by the standards of his own time. It says Cromwell's actions can be partly justified in the following ways:

1   The Ulster killings of 1641

The English hated the Catholic Irish because they believed they had massacred many thousands of Protestants in Ulster when the rebellion began in 1641 (source 7). Like most English people,

SOURCE 7

The killing of Irish Protestants by Catholics in 1641. Propaganda pictures such as this caused the English to believe that the Catholics planned and carried out a wholesale massacre of Protestants. Although about 3,000 Protestants were murdered during the uprising, there was no massacre and no plan for one. The Protestants quickly retaliated for the murders.

Cromwell believed the Irish should be punished for this. He told Irish Catholic priests:

SOURCE 8

You, unprovoked, put the English to the most unheard of and most barbarous massacre (without respect of sex or age) that ever the sun beheld.

Declaration to the Irish Catholic clergy, 1650

2   The rules of war

Everyone in the seventeenth century accepted that there were special rules of war in the case of a siege. First, the attacking commander had to summon, or order, the town to surrender. If the defending commander refused and the town was then captured by breaking down the walls and storming in, the defenders could be killed. If the town surrendered before the walls were broken through, the defenders were given 'quarter' – that is, they were spared. These rules were intended to encourage towns to surrender quickly in order to avoid the bloodshed that resulted from an attack.

Cromwell did summon Drogheda to surrender. Sir Arthur Aston, its commander, refused the summons. Cromwell then ordered the defenders to be given no quarter. He did not directly order women, children or priests to be killed; but civilians were bound to be caught up in the confusion.

3   Preventing further bloodshed

Cromwell believed the killings would would save further bloodshed by persuading other towns to surrender. After the siege he said the killings:

SOURCE 9

Will tend to prevent the effusion [spilling] of blood for the future.
Cromwell, Letter to the Speaker of Parliament, 17 September, 1649

After this, several towns did give in without a fight. Cromwell therefore made a correct military decision.

Different interpretations: the hard judgement

This interpretation says that Cromwell should be condemned, even by the standards of his own time. The reasons are:

1   The Irish: a non-people?

Cromwell did not think of the Irish as human beings with rights. He treated them differently from other enemies, for example the Scots.

His feelings about punishing the Irish for the Ulster killings of 1641 caused him to view all Irish people in the same way and make no distinction between soldiers and civilians. He was out for revenge. After Drogheda there was another masssacre at Wexford which he did not order, but did not stop either. He said the families killed had been:

i **Atomic bombs** *The Second World War (1939–45) involved every powerful country in the world. On one side were the Allied Powers, chiefly Britain, France, Poland, the USA and the USSR. On the other were the Axis powers of Germany, Japan and Italy. During the war the USA's programme to develop bombs using nuclear energy led to the invention of the atomic bomb. By May 1945 Italy and Germany had surrendered, but Japan fought on in the Pacific. In August 1945 while US troops were preparing to invade Japan, the US President, Harry S. Truman ordered the US Air Force to drop an atomic bomb on the Japanese city of Hiroshima. Most of the city was destroyed and over 200,000 people died. Three days later a second bomb was dropped on the city of Nagasaki. Japan surrendered on 14 August 1945.*

SOURCE 10

Made with their bloods to answer [pay for] the cruelties which they had exercised [carried out] upon the lives of . . . poor Protestants.

Cromwell, letter to the Speaker of the Parliament of England, 14 October 1649

He went on to say that since there were now so many empty homes, it would be a good idea for Protestant colonists to go and settle there. He appeared to have no feeling for the victims' suffering. In another letter, he wrote with horror about the things Catholics did to Protestants; but he showed no sense of horror at the actions of his own soldiers.

2 The rules of war

The rules about sieges were not always applied. Cromwell could have given quarter if he had wanted to. He certainly ought to have stopped the killing of civilians. He probably would have done if they had not been Irish.

3 The wrong way to prevent bloodshed

Cromwell's argument that the killings saved more lives later is the same argument used to justify dropping two **atomic bombs** on Japanese cities in 1945 in order to end the Second World War. But, is it ever justifiable to kill civilians for such a purpose? In any case, some towns still did not surrender even after Drogheda.

The Republic

After the execution of Charles I in 1649, the Rump Parliament (source 11) abolished the monarchy and the House of Lords and declared England to be a commonwealth, or republic. It remained one until 1660. There were several different governments during the time of the Republic (source 12), but in the end government without the Crown collapsed. In 1660 Charles II was invited to return to become king. Monarchy was restored, and that event is known as the 'Restoration'.

SOURCE 11

The Great Seal of England, 1651, showing the Rump Parliament. In 1653 representatives from Ireland and Scotland sat in Parliament for the first time. This continued throughout the Protectorate (see source 12).

SOURCE 12

The governments of the Republic. The period 1649–60 is also known as the Interregnum, which is Latin for 'between the reigns'.

Rump Parliament

The Rump both made the laws and ran the day-to-day business of government through a council of State chosen from its own members. It was dismissed in 1653 by Cromwell and the army.

Barebone's Parliament

Named after one of its members, Praise-God Barebone, a London leather seller. Its members were not elected. Instead Cromwell and army officers chose about 140 puritans who they hoped would rule wisely, helped by God. Some members did not agree with the army. After six months the majority of members voted to dissolve, or end, the Parliament and to hand power back to the army.

Protectorate

Oliver Cromwell was made Lord Protector. He ruled with the help of a Council of State and Parliament, which had to meet regularly. Royalists were not allowed to vote. Parliament offered Cromwell the crown in 1657, but he refused it. He died in 1658 and was succeeded as Protector by his son, Richard, who quarrelled with army officers and resigned in 1659.

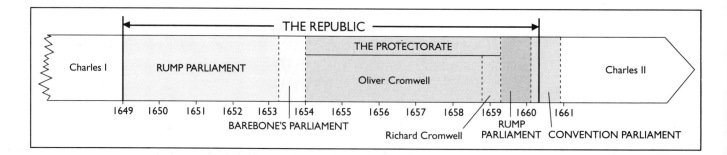

ℹ️ **Convention** A convention is an assembly or gathering of people. The word was applied to the 1660 Parliament to show that it was not a Parliament summoned by the Crown.

Rump Parliament, 1659

The Rump was re-called by the army, and then quarrelled with it. General Monk, in command of the English forces in Scotland, marched his army south and persuaded Parliament to dissolve itself and order an election for a new Parliament. Royalists were allowed to vote again.

Convention Parliament, 1660

This consisted of Lords and Commons. A large majority were in favour of restoring the monarchy. They voted for government to be in the hands of the Crown, Lords and Commons and then invited Charles II to return as king.

Why was the Crown restored in 1660?

From 1649 onwards, both support for a monarchy and opposition to Cromwell and the army grew. In the end, only Cromwell held the Republic together. His death opened the way to the Restoration.

The Crown gained supporters

The Royalists

The execution of the King meant that Parliament and the Royalists could never make up their quarrel. Royalists were not allowed to vote or help govern their localities. So, they were always hostile to the Republic and waiting for a chance to restore Charles II.

Charles the martyr

Charles acted with courage and dignity at his trial and execution. Many people felt sympathy for him. By killing him, Parliament made him a martyr for his cause. His trial and execution reminded people that Parliament was now ruling by force. If the King could be executed without a proper trial, who else was safe?

Moderate Parliamentarians

The moderate Parliamentarians were those who had fought against the King in the war, but expected to negotiate a peace with him. They were horrified by the execution of the King.

Cromwell and the army made enemies

The Levellers

These were soldiers in the New Model Army, mostly yeomen or craftsmen, who hoped Parliament's victory would lead to big changes in society. They wanted a republic in which men over twenty-one, except servants and beggars, could vote. When the Rump rejected their ideas they mutinied. Cromwell thought Leveller ideas threatened the power of country gentlemen like himself. He put the revolt down by force. After this, the Levellers hated Cromwell.

Fear of religious freedom

SOURCE 13

A Quaker meeting. Quakers believed the spirit of God was within each person. This often caused them to tremble or quake during their meetings – hence their name. They did not believe in priests or parish churches. They did not accept the ranks in society and refused to take off their hats as a mark of respect to their social superiors.

activity

1a How does source 13 and the information in the text about the Levellers suggest that the Civil War caused ordinary people to put forward new ideas about (i) religion, (ii) politics, (iii) society?
b Why might these ideas worry the country gentlemen?
c How does source 13 suggest that women were important in the Quaker movement?

Cromwell and the army did not want the Presbyterian Church which Parliament had set up in place of the Church of England in 1646. They wanted a national Church in which all Protestants could worship how they pleased. That meant each parish or religious group would be free to run its own affairs.

This was a new and very unpopular idea. Country gentlemen who were Presbyterians and those who supported the old Church of England disagreed with it. They were frightened of the many new religious groups that had grown up since the Civil War, such as the Quakers (source 13). They thought people who were allowed to worship how they pleased would want to behave as they pleased in other ways. They wanted a Church that disciplined the people.

Hatred of the rule of force

Although people put up with Cromwell's rule, they disliked it because it was based on force (source 14), not on agreement. Once, when Parliament would not grant the taxes Cromwell wanted, he

SOURCE 14

Cromwell and his soldiers dismiss the Rump in 1653. Cromwell and the army believed the Rump was not interested in changes such as freedom of worship. The Rump argued that the army should serve Parliament and not the other way round.

activity

2 Look at source 14 and the information in the text and source 1, Part 6 and the information on pages 66–67. What was **a** similar, **b** different about Cromwell's dismissal of the Rump and Charles I's attempt to arrest the five members?
3a Suggest some reasons why the army did not want Cromwell to become king.
b Cromwell thought very hard before he refused to accept the crown. What do you think his arguments might have been (i) for, (ii) against accepting it?

used the power of the army to order people to pay anyway. Another time, he divided the country into eleven areas and appointed a major-general to govern each one.

In 1657, Parliament offered Cromwell the crown, thinking that if he was king he would have to rule according to the old laws and not by force. The army did not like the idea and Cromwell refused.

Cromwell's death

Even though the army had made so many enemies, very few people actually wanted to go back to a monarchy while Cromwell was alive. Cromwell knew that the Protectorate would not succeed unless more people supported it. He tried to make friends again with the moderate Parliamentarians and even with some Royalists.

The country gentlemen disagreed with many of his opinions, but liked the fact that he kept the country peaceful. When Cromwell died, there was no one strong enough to take his place, so republican government collapsed.

The Restoration

SOURCE 15

Charles II's coronation procession, painted by Dick Stoop.

There was great rejoicing when Charles II returned, and his coronation brought back all the splendour and pageantry of the monarchy (source 15).

Charles II wanted to heal the wounds in society caused by the Civil Wars and the Republic. He pardoned everyone who had fought against his father, except those who had actually signed his death warrant in 1649. He invited Royalists, Parliamentarians and old supporters of Cromwell to serve on the Privy Council and as Justices of the Peace.

The Civil War had been fought to try to control the powers of the Crown and to make sure that there was a Church with which Puritans could agree. Did the Civil War and Republic make any difference?

Government

The Crown

The powers of the Crown were restored completely in England and Wales, Ireland and Scotland. Charles II's reign was declared to have started from the moment of his father's death. All the Acts of Parliament to which Charles I had agreed stayed, but all those passed in the Republic were declared to have no force.

SOURCE 16

Charles II touching for the king's evil. Many people suffered from a disease of the neck glands called scrofula. It was known as the 'king's evil' because it was believed that the monarch had a power, given by God, to cure it by touching the victim. Charles II held the ceremony more often than any of his predecessors.

activity

1 Look at source 16.
a How does it suggest that people believed the monarch possessed miraculous powers?
b What does it tell you about Charles II's beliefs about kingship?
c Suggest some reasons why he chose to hold the ceremony so often.
2 How do sources 15 and 16 help to explain the popularity of the Restoration among ordinary people?

This meant that the Crown could no longer raise taxes on its own, through methods such as Ship Money, because Charles I had agreed to Acts of Parliament forbidding that in 1641. But it remained in charge of the militia and continued to appoint its own advisers.

Parliament

Parliament played exactly the same part in government after 1660 as it had done before the Civil War. It advised the King, made laws and was asked to agree to the Crown raising taxes. In 1664, even the Act which had been passed in 1641, saying Parliament had to meet every three years, was changed so that it was more vague and possible for the monarch to ignore.

Ireland and Scotland were no longer united with England and Wales through having their own members in the Parliament at Westminster. Instead, the Irish Parliament started to sit again in Dublin and the Scottish Parliament met again in Edinburgh.

Religion

The Church of England

The Church of England was restored along with the Crown. Charles II wanted it to be the sort of Church most Puritans could accept, as they had done in the time of Elizabeth I. He also wanted to allow those Roman Catholics and Puritans who could not accept it the right to worship in their own way.

The Parliament elected in 1662, called the Cavalier Parliament because of its very traditional royalist opinions, refused to accept these ideas. In 1662 Charles had to agree to an Act of Uniformity which forced priests to take tests to prove they agreed with the Prayer Book. About 2,000 failed because of their Puritan opinions and either left or were thrown out of their parishes. The Church of England was never again a truly national Church to which nearly everyone could belong.

Dissenters and Catholics

Protestants who would not accept the Church of England were called Dissenters because they dissented from it – that is, disagreed with it. Dissenters included Presbyterians and many of the groups Cromwell wanted to protect, such as the Quakers. Parliament passed Acts which prevented Dissenters and Catholics from holding their own services and from having any job in local or national government. They became second-class citizens.

Scotland

During the Civil War the Scots, who had signed the Covenant in 1638 to protect the Kirk against Charles I, set up a fully Presbyterian Kirk without bishops. Bishops were brought back at the Restoration, but each parish was left to decide whether or not to use the Prayer Book. About 270 Covenanting ministers, so called because they still supported the Covenant, refused to accept bishops and were dismissed.

Many Covenanting ministers then started to hold their own open-air services, called 'conventicles' (source 17). The Scottish Parliament passed Acts against them and government troops were sent to hunt them down. They were defeated in two pitched battles and many were either sent abroad or executed.

activity

1 How does source 17 suggest that Dissenters in Scotland came from a wide variety of social backgrounds?

2 Look at source 13 and the information in the text on pages 89–90 and 93. Why would Oliver Cromwell have been particularly unhappy about the arrangements for religion made after the Restoration?

SOURCE 17

A conventicle of Scottish dissenters.

Were the Puritans killjoys?

SOURCE 18

An early seventeenth-century theatre. Find:
- the stage, open on three sides
- the audience standing around the edge of the stage and sitting in galleries above. The theatre was circular in shape
- various characters from the plays. The two at the front left are from **William Shakespeare**'s *Henry IV Parts 1 and 2.*

activity

1 Look at sources 18 and 19.
a How were theatres built after 1660 different from those built earlier?
b Was anything the same?

i   William Shakespeare *(1564–1616) is probably the world's most famous playwright. In 1594 he became an actor and playwright for a company of actors in London. He later became part owner of the Globe and Blackfriars Theatres. He wrote 38 plays and many poems.*

The popular opinion about the Puritans is that they were gloomy people. They disapproved of the arts, especially the theatre. They had no fun themselves and stopped other people having it too, particularly during the time of the Republic when they were the rulers. When Charles II returned, artists of all sorts flourished and the fun in life came back again. How true is this? Decide for yourself whether or not you think the Puritans were killjoys.

The theatre

The theatre was popular among all classes of the population in the late sixteenth and early seventeenth centuries (source 18). Puritan writers said plays taught audiences bad and immoral behaviour

SOURCE 19

A late seventeenth-century theatre. Find:
- the stage
- the arch at the front of the stage. It is called a 'proscenium arch'
- the painted cloth at the back of the stage
- the galleries for the audience. The audience also sat on seats in front of the stage.

i **Opera**   *This was* The Siege of Rhodes *by Sir William Davenant, performed in 1656. It was possibly the first English opera.*

i **John Milton**   *John Milton (1608–74) wrote poems and a play in the 1630s and political pamphlets in the 1640s. He attacked bishops and defended divorce and a free press, saying that people should be allowed to write and print what they pleased. He disagreed with the rules Parliament made to stop this. In 1649 he wrote a defence of the execution of the King, and became Latin Secretary to the Council of State. He started to go blind and had to write with the help of secretaries. In retirement, after the Restoration, he wrote the two long poems for which he is most famous,* Paradise Lost *(published 1667) and* Paradise Regained *(1671).*

i **Andrew Marvell**   *Andrew Marvell (1621–78) was tutor to the Cromwell and Fairfax families, a member of Parliament and assistant to Milton as Latin Secretary to the Council of State. His poems are full of wit and humour. After the Restoration he continued to argue for a republic and wrote satires to make fun of the weaknesses of Charles II and his ministers.*

because they were always about people who lied, cheated, swore, tried to make love to each other, or killed each other:

SOURCE 20

If you will learn . . . to contemn [despise] God . . . and to commit all kinds of sin and mischief, you need to go to no other school, for . . . these you may see painted before your eyes in . . . plays.

Philip Stubbes, *The Anatomie of Abuses*, 1583

When the Civil War started in 1642, Parliament ordered theatres to shut. This was partly because Parliamentarians thought they might be places where Royalists would meet together and plot, and also because they feared some plays might be used to criticise them. During the Republic some plays were probably performed in secret and one **opera** was shown in public. The theatres did not open again until 1660 (source 19).

Dancing, music and poetry

Some Puritans attacked dancing:

SOURCE 21

It withdraws young gentlewomen from their studies to the dancing school . . . from their needles and suchlike honest employments, and for the most part makes them idle housewives, whores or spendthrifts ever after.

William Prynne, *Histriomastix*, 1634

But, the celebrations for the wedding of Oliver Cromwell's daughter in 1657 went on until the early hours of the morning and involved:

SOURCE 22

Much mirth with frolics [laughter and merry-making], besides mixed dancing.

Quoted in B. Coward, *Oliver Cromwell*, 1991

The celebrations also included music from forty-eight violins and fifty trumpets. Cromwell and many other Puritans were well known for their love of music. Music making at home was a very popular pastime after the Restoration (source 23) but it always had been – and as much among Puritans as anyone else.

Cromwell also took an interest in poetry. Two well-known poets who were also Puritans were **John Milton** and **Andrew Marvell**, both of whom worked as secretaries to the Council of State in the Republic.

activity

I Look at source 24. What objections do you think Puritans might have to the games shown here?

2a What impression does source 21 give of the Puritans' attitude to dancing?

b How does source 22 alter that impression?

3 Which sources and pieces of information on pages 95–97 suggest the Puritans:

a were killjoys;

b were not killjoys;

c did not like the arts;

d did like the arts?

SOURCE 23

A group of musicians in the early eighteenth century.

SOURCE 24

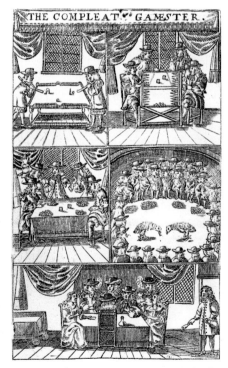

The Compleate Gamster, first published in 1674 as an instruction book for games. These games became even more popular after the Restoration because they had been forbidden in the time of the Republic.

Sports and pastimes

All Puritans disapproved of gambling, and of sports and games being played on Sundays. During the Republic they banned race-meetings, cock fights and bear baiting. They stopped Maypole dancing and celebrations at Christmas. They closed ale-houses.

One of the reasons why Cromwell tried the experiment of appointing major-generals to run areas of the country was to see if they could enforce these rules, and make people behave in what Cromwell and the Puritans called a more 'godly' way.

Ordinary people were very fond of their sports and pastimes, and greeted the Restoration with delight. This was partly because it meant they could go back to their old games and festivals (source 24).

assignments

I Use the sources and information on pages 80–82 and 89–91.
a Describe two causes and two consequences of the execution of Charles I.
b Say which cause and which consequence you think were the most important. Explain your reasons.

2 Use the sources and information about Cromwell at Drogheda (pages 84–87).
a Organise a class discussion about the strengths and weaknesses of (i) the soft judgement, and (ii) the hard judgement on Cromwell.
b In Ireland today, popular opinion agrees with the hard judgement on Cromwell. Explain why you think that is.

3a Use the sources and information in Part 7 to describe (i) political causes and consequences, and (ii) religious causes and consequences of the failure of the Republic.
b Organise a class discussion to talk about whether you think the (i) political, or (ii) religious causes were most important in causing the Republic to fail.

4a Use the sources and information in Parts 6 and 7 to make charts or displays to show for each of these dates: 1641; 1649–53; 1653–58; 1660–62:
  (i) the powers of the Crown;
 (ii) the powers of Parliament;
(iii) religious arrangements.
b What do you think (i) changed, and (ii) stayed the same in each of these areas in
● the short-term,
● the long-term?
c How much change do you think happened because of the Civil War?

5a Look at source 21 and the sources and information on the theatre (page 95) and sports and pastimes (page 97). What impression of the Puritans' attitude to (i) popular pastimes, (ii) the arts do these give you?
b How do the remaining sources and information on dancing, music and poetry change that impression?
c What do you think are the strengths and weaknesses of the interpretations that say the Puritans were (i) killjoys, (ii) not interested in the arts?
d In what respects is the popular view of the Puritans as killjoys incorrect?

8
Science and Superstition

In Part 8 you can investigate how people's ideas about the world changed between 1500 and 1750. The first section, Science, is about changes in the way scholars thought about how the world works. The second section, Witchcraft, is about beliefs which both educated and uneducated people held in 1500. In 1750 some people no longer held those beliefs, but others still hung on to them.

Science

Let us start by looking at the differences in the way scholars thought about the world in 1500 and 1750.

The world in 1500

The universe

The universe means the earth, the heavens and everything that is in them. In 1500 scholars' ideas about how the universe worked were based on the theories of Ptolemy who lived in the second century (source 1, page 100). They thought the earth was the centre of the universe and the sun and planets moved round it in circles.

They thought the sun and the planets were part of a separate, heavenly, world where no substance changed because it was perfect. They thought the earth was made up of materials that could change because they were not perfect.

Nature

People's ideas about nature were based on those of the Greek scholar **Aristotle**. They believed every substance on earth was made up of a mixture of four 'elements'. There were two heavy elements, earth and water; and two light ones, air and fire.

They thought objects moved according to the elements in them – so smoke moved upwards because it was airy and light, and stones

i **Aristotle** Aristotle (384–322 BC) was a Greek philosopher who taught and wrote about a very wide range of subjects which included logic, politics, poetry, biology and physics. After the fall of the Roman Empire, his work was lost in Europe, though it was still well-known to Arab and Jewish scholars. They re-introduced it to Europe in the 13th century.

SOURCE 1

Ptolemy's universe, from an atlas of 1661. Find:
- the earth in the centre with its elements of earth, water, air and fire
- the sun and the planets circling the earth.

moved downwards because they were earthy and heavy. If a substance changed, it was because the balance of the elements in it had changed.

Alchemists

Alchemists (source 2) thought substances such as stones and metals had a special power inside that could change them for the better. For example, they thought ordinary metals had the power to become gold, if only someone could find a way of releasing the right forces.

SOURCE 2

Alchemists at work.

The world in 1750

In 1750 scholars no longer thought substances were made up of the elements of earth, water, air and fire. Instead, they thought they were probably made up of tiny particles. They no longer thought it was possible to turn another metal into gold.

Scholars also believed that the earth went round the sun and not the other way round. They no longer thought the sun and the planets were part of a separate, heavenly world.

They thought of the universe – sun, planets and everything on earth – as one big machine that worked according to definite rules, like a clock. They compared God to a clockmaker and said the universe worked according to the rules God had made. As they found out more about the way the universe worked, they said they were showing God's power and wisdom as its designer and maker.

activity

1a Use sources 1 and 2 and the information in the text on pages 99–101 to make lists of scholars' ideas about
- the universe,
- nature

in (i) 1500, (ii) 1750.

b Copy this chart and enter the information from your lists on it as the example shows.

	In 1500	In 1750
Ideas about the universe	The earth was the centre of the universe	The sun was the centre of the universe
Ideas about nature		

How did these changes in ideas take place?

Mathematics

In the sixteenth and seventeenth centuries, scholars invented new ways of doing mathematics. Some of them made discoveries mainly because they were very clever at doing difficult calculations.

In 1543, the Polish astronomer Nicolaus Copernicus used mathematics to work out that the sun, not the earth, was the centre of the universe (source 3, page 102). He proved that the earth and all the other planets moved around the sun and that the moon moved around the earth.

activity

I Look at sources I and 3.
a What were the differences between the ideas about the universe of Ptolemy and Copernicus?
b Was anything the same?

SOURCE 3

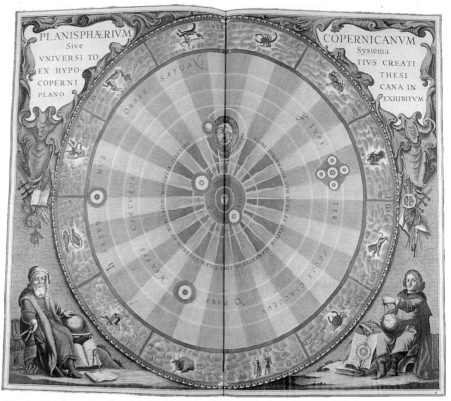

The universe according to Copernicus, from an atlas of 1661. Find:
- the sun at the centre
- the planets, including the earth, circling the sun
- the moon circling the earth
- four planets circling Jupiter. Copernicus did not know about these. They were first seen through a telescope by Galileo in the seventeenth century
- the signs of the zodiac around the edge. Many people believed the planets affected events on earth.

In 1687, an English mathematician called Isaac Newton worked out that the same rules governed both the way planets move in the heavens and the way things such as stones fall back to earth when they are thrown up in the air.

Observation and experiment

In the sixteenth and seventeeth centuries, scientists started to look carefully at things to see how they worked, instead of relying on ancient theories. Then they started to carry out experiments to see if their own theories could be proved or not.

In the sixteenth century, doctors started to dissect, or cut up, bodies to find out how they worked. In the early seventeenth century, a doctor called William Harvey used dissection, observation and experiment to prove that blood, pumped by the heart, circulates right round the body (source 4). Till then, doctors thought it probably moved backwards and forwards.

Harvey's discovery led to important medical discoveries and new ways of treating patients over the next 300 years. But it made no

SOURCE 4

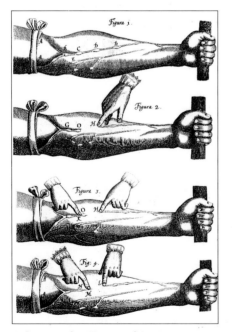

A diagram by Harvey showing an experiment to prove that veins contain one-way valves and, therefore, that the blood must go right round the body in one direction.

> **i** **Robert Boyle** *developed a pump to create a vacuum. He used small animals to prove that air is necessary to support life. In another experiment he hung a watch with an alarm in a vacuum jar. When the alarm went off, no one could hear it. This proved that sound does not carry within a vacuum.*

> **i** **Bubonic plague** known in the Middle Ages as the Black Death, broke out throughout the 16th and early 17th centuries, particularly in London. The last and greatest outbreak took place in 1665 and killed 70,000–100,000 people. The plague germs lived in fleas which in turn lived on black rats. After 1665, black rats began to die out while brown rats, which did not carry the fleas, increased in number. From then on outbreaks of bubonic plague were very rare.

activity

2 Would a seventeenth-century patient have described Harvey's discovery as 'progress'? Explain your reasons.

3 Look at source 6. How do you think the use of the microscope helped scientists to challenge Aristotle's ideas about the elements?

4 Look at source 7 and the information in the text on page 102. How did **a** Galileo, **b** Newton help to disprove the idea that the planets were in a heavenly world separate from the earth?

difference at all to the way sick people were treated in the seventeenth century. Doctors remained ignorant of the causes of most diseases, including the **bubonic plague** which continued to kill thousands of people in the sixteenth and seventeenth centuries.

Robert Boyle, the youngest son of the Earl of Cork in Ireland, carried out many experiments on air. In 1661 he wrote a book to show that the idea that everything was made up of the four elements of earth, fire, air and water was wrong.

Inventions

Telescopes were invented at the start of the seventeenth century and microscopes (source 5) in the middle of the century. Now scientists could look closely at large objects far away, such as the planets, and very small objects closer to home, such as fleas (source 6).

SOURCE 5

A late seventeenth-century microscope. Until recently, this was thought to be Robert Hooke's own microscope. As well as working with the microscope, Hooke made studies of the weather and the nature of light.

SOURCE 6

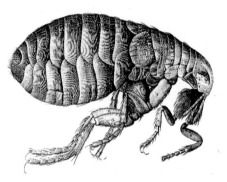

Hooke's drawing of a flea under a microscope, 1665.

In 1610 the Italian astronomer Galileo Galilei's observations through a telescope helped scholars to understand that the planets were not part of a separate, perfect, world:

SOURCE 7

The moon is not smooth, uniform [all the same], but rough, full of cavities [holes], like the face of the earth.

Galileo Galilei, *Starry Messenger*, 1610

Robert Boyle's experiments on air were only possible because of the invention of the air pump.

Communication

SOURCE 8

Charles II as Patron of the Royal Society, painted in 1684. Charles took an interest in all the new ideas and inventions of his time, particularly those to do with ships. He encouraged members of the Society to invent new methods of shipbuilding, gunnery and navigation.

> **i** **The Great Fire** *broke out in a baker's shop in London on 2 September, 1666. It lasted for three days and destroyed about four-fifths of the city, including over 13,000 houses and 87 churches. Only 20 people died. After the fire, three members of the Royal Society – Wren, Hooke and Evelyn – each presented Charles II with different plans for rebuilding the City of London in a formal way. None was carried out because many landowners refused to co-operate. So, Wren often had to fit his new churches onto very small sites.*

> **i** **Patron** Someone who helps and protects a person or an organisation.

SOURCE 9

Sir Christopher Wren. Find:
- the globe of the heavens and the telescope. Wren was a professor of astronomy before he was thirty
- the mathematical instruments. He was also interested in mathematics and geometry
- the plan of St Paul's Cathedral. After the **Great Fire** of London (1666) he became an architect and built a new St Paul's to replace the one that burned down
- the skyline of London in the background. As well as St Paul's, Wren re-built fifty-two parish churches. Their spires became well-known landmarks.

During the Civil War and Republic, a group of scientists began to meet reguarly in Oxford and London. Most, such as Christopher Wren (source 9), worked in many fields of knowledge. In 1660 they asked Charles II to agree to them forming the Royal Society. Charles agreed and became its **patron** (source 8). The support of the King gave scientists great encouragement.

The Royal Society held regular meetings and its members wrote about their ideas and experiments. This meant that scientists could learn from and help each other, so ideas changed more quickly. Hooke, Boyle and Newton all belonged to the Royal Society.

Members of the Society also met with inventors and craftspeople, and some of their ideas were used in a practical way in machines. Robert Hooke invented a spring-balance which was used in clocks (source 10).

SOURCE 10

Thomas Tompion's year-going spring clock, made for King William III sometime between 1695 and 1700. Tompion was born in Bedfordshire and went to London in 1671. There he met Robert Hooke and tried out his ideas for improving clocks and watches, including the use of a spring-balance. The case of this clock is made of silver and ebony.

Did anything stay the same?

Astrology

In 1500 both scholars and uneducated people believed the stars and planets affected life on earth. Astrologers studied the movement of the stars and planets to try to foretell what was going to happen. They published their predictions in almanacs (source 11).

In 1750 scientists no longer believed in astrology, but many educated and most uneducated people still did. Almanacs were the most popular type of book in the country.

SOURCE 11

AN
ALMANACK
OR
PROGNOSTICATION for the year of our LORD 1658, Being the second after Bissextile or Leap year. Calculated for the Meridian of London, and may indifferently serve for England, Scotland, and Ireland.

By SARAH JINNER Student in Astrology.

London, Printed by J. Streater for the Company of Stationers.

An almanac. There were over 2,000 separate versions in the seventeenth century. As well as astrological predictions, almanacs contained practical information, such as calendars, details of fairs and notes on medicine and farming.

activity

1 Look at sources 5 and 10, and the information in the text.
a How did (i) inventors and craftspeople help scientists, (ii) scientists help inventors and craftspeople?
b Suggest some ways in which you think science, invention and craft are linked. Explain your ideas.

Witchcraft

activity

1 Look at source 12.
a Do you think that if Elizabeth's parents had understood the medical reasons for her death, they would have accused Susan of being a witch?
b What does this tell you about why people blamed things on witches?
2 Look at source 14. What innocent reasons might an old woman have for keeping pets?

Witches and warlocks

Ordinary people had always believed in magic. They believed wise women and wizards had the power to heal illnesses and stop bad things happening by using charms and spells. They also believed the devil spent his time trying to cause evil in the world. Witches and warlocks were women and men who made deals with the devil and helped his work by causing harm to other people.

Witch trials

Witchcraft was not seen as a particularly serious matter until 1542 when it became punishable by death. From 1563 to 1736 witchcraft that caused a person's death was punishable by death, but lesser forms of witchcraft, such as using it to injure someone, were punishable by imprisonment.

Between 1542 and 1685, when the last witchcraft trial was held, many women were accused of being witches, but very few men were accused of being warlocks. People accused women of killing and hurting animals; of spoiling their crops or their efforts to make butter, cheese and beer; of causing illness, accidents and quarrels amongst neighbours; and of causing death:

SOURCE 12

Susan Pickenden of Halden, spinster [spinner], wife of John Pickenden of Halden, labourer, on 28 October 1648 ... bewitched Elizabeth Lowes, daughter of William Lowes, aged about 17 years, who languished until 8 March following, when she died ...

Quoted in C. L'Estange Ewen ed., *Witch Hunting and Witch Trials*, 1929

How to tell a witch

You could tell a witch because she always had one or more 'familiars' (source 13), which were spirits or imps which took the form of small animals:

SOURCE 14

Mary Hockett of Ramsey, widow ... did entertain three evil spirits each in the likeness of a mouse, called 'Littleman', 'Prettyman' and 'Daynty'.

Quoted in C. L'Estange Ewen ed., *Witch Hunting and Witch Trials*, 1929

SOURCE 13

Witches being watched by Matthew Hopkins. He rode round East Anglia with two assistants between 1644 and 1647 organising the detection of witches in return for a fee. This picture is from Hopkins's book, *The Discovery of Witches*, published in 1647.

A witch also carried a spot or unusual mark on her body as a sign of her pact with the devil. The way to prove someone was a witch was to 'swim' them (source 15).

SOURCE 15

Swimming a suspected witch. The woman was stripped, her left thumb tied to her right toe and her right thumb to her left toe, and then she was thrown into the water. If she floated she was guilty; if she sank she was innocent, but very often drowned.

According to a book on witchcraft it was easy to spot witches because they were:

SOURCE 16

Commonly old, lame, bleare-eyed, pale, foul and full of wrinkles . . . lean and deformed, showing meloncholy in their faces . . . doting, scolds, mad, divelish.

Reginald Scot, *Discoverie of Witchcraft*, 1584

A Huntingdonshire vicar who thought all this was nonsense wrote:

SOURCE 17

Every old woman with a wrinkled face, a furrowed brow, a hairy lip . . . a squint eye, a squeaking voice or a scolding tongue, having . . . a dog or cat by her side, is not only suspected but pronounced for [said to be] a witch.

John Gaule, 1645

activity

3 Look at sources 16 and 17 and the information in the text about witch trials. How do they support the idea that people accused women of being witches if **a** they were old, **b** they were poor, **c** they looked odd, **d** the accusers felt guilty about them, **e** they were perfectly normal really?

activity

I Look at source 18 and the information in the text.
a How does it show that some people's ideas about witches took longer to change than others?
b Who do you think changed their minds
(i) quickest, (ii) slowest? Explain your reasons.

The opinion of historians

Historians who have studied witch trials say that in a typical case the accused woman was old and poor. The people who accused her were better off and had turned her away when she turned up begging at the door. After that, some misfortune happened in the house and the accusers blamed it on the old 'witch'.

The end of witch trials

By the eighteenth century, educated people no longer believed in witchcraft, and the laws against it were ended in 1736. Even so, in 1751 Ruth Osborne was put to the swimming test in Tring in Hertfordshire. She drowned and a chimney-sweep who had helped with the swimming was hanged for her murder. According to a bystander at his execution, the crowd grumbled that:

SOURCE 18

It was a hard case to hang a man for destroying an old wicked woman who had done so much harm by her witchcraft.

Quoted in J. A. Sharpe, *Early Modern England 1550–1760*, 1967

assignments

1a Make a chart or display to show how ideas about the universe and nature (i) changed, (ii) stayed the same between 1500 and 1750.
b The changes in ideas happened because of changes in (i) the way scientists worked, (ii) inventions, (iii) communication between scientists. Give some examples of each of these kinds of change and write a few sentences about each one.

2 Harvey's discovery about the circulation of the blood changed seventeenth-century scientists' understanding about the workings of the human body, but it did not improve the way patients were treated in the seventeenth century.
a How does this show that change and progress are not the same?
b Look at source 4 and the information in the text. Do you think (i) a seventeenth-century scientist, (ii) a patient today would describe his discovery as progress? Explain your reasons.
c What else does this tell you about change and progress?

3a How did the ideas and beliefs of the following groups of people about the working of the universe and witchcraft change between 1500 and 1750 and in what ways did they stay the same? Use the sources and information in Part 8.
  (i) scientists and scholars;
  (ii) educated people who were not scientists and scholars;
(iii) uneducated people
b What does this tell you about (i) rates of change, and (ii) the ways in which patterns of change can be complicated?

An invitation to invade

On 5 November 1688, England was invaded. Prince William of Orange, the ruler of the Dutch Republic, landed at Brixham in Devon with 12,000 troops (source 1). But this was an invasion with a difference. William had been invited to invade by a large group of leading English landowners who were dissatisfied with the rule of King James II (source 2, page 110).

There was no battle and no bloodshed. James II left the country and the Parliaments of England and Scotland invited William and his wife Mary, who was James's daughter, to become king and queen of the two countries. These extraordinary events became known as the 'Glorious Revolution' and they probably had more effect on the government of England, Wales, Scotland and Ireland than all the years of the Civil War and Republic.

SOURCE 1

William of Orange landing at Brixham in 1688. The same wind that blew William's fleet down the Channel towards Devon trapped James II's fleet off the Thames estuary. Afterwards people called it the 'Protestant wind'.

activity

I How does source 2 suggest James was a successful commander?

i **Whigs** and **Tories** These were nicknames. 'Whig' came from 'whiggamor', a 'cattle-driver' – a 17th-century term of abuse for Scottish Presbyterians. 'Tory' came from the Irish word 'toraighe' – a 'pursuer'. The name was given to 17th-century Irish outlaws. It came to mean any Irish Catholic or Royalist.

Why were William and Mary invited to become king and queen?

When Charles II died in 1685 he had no legitimate children to succeed him (though he was proud of having at least fourteen illegitimate ones), so his brother James, Duke of York, became king. There were all the usual celebrations for a new monarch, yet, three years later, no one supported him when William invaded. What went wrong?

Whigs and Tories

When Charles II was still king, James announced that he had become a Roman Catholic. Members of Parliament split into two groups over this. One group, who became known as **Whigs**, wanted to pass an Act to stop James being allowed to become king. The other group, known as **Tories**, believed that monarchs were responsible for the way they ruled to God, not to their people. They believed that the people, and therefore Parliament, did not have the right to interfere with the line of succession. This idea was called 'Divine Right'.

Between them, Charles II and the Tories defeated the Whigs' plans. James II succeeded peacefully and promised to defend the Church of England, which was what the Tories cared about most of all. As long as he did this, they were happy for his private beliefs to be his own affair.

SOURCE 2

James VII of Scotland and II England, painted by Sir Godfrey Kneller in 1684–5. Before he became king, James had a very successful career as a soldier and as an admiral in the navy.

The laws against Catholics

James believed that if the laws against Catholics were abolished, so that they could worship freely and hold government jobs, thousands of people would want to become Catholics again of their own free will. He did not understand that people still saw Catholics as enemies and that they feared the restoration of the Pope's authority.

James found that Parliament would not help him. Whigs and Tories were united in not wishing to change the laws against Catholics.

i **Louis XIV** *Louis XIV was king of France from 1634 to 1715. He believed in Divine Right and ruled as if his word was law. He fought several wars to enlarge the territory of France. He was the patron of artists, writers and architects and built a magnificent palace at Versailles. Because of the splendour of his Court, he is often called the Sun King.*

The powers of the Crown

James decided to act on his own. The Crown had the power to override laws under special circumstances. James used this power. First, he allowed Catholics to become officers in the army and take jobs in local and national government.

Then, he announced that Catholics and Dissenters could worship freely and hold government jobs. He hoped that in return Dissenters in Parliament would help him to change the law against freedom of worship. He started to change the rules for Parliamentary elections in towns to make sure that Dissenters would be elected.

People were frightened. If the King could override laws on religion, what was to stop him overriding all laws?

The succession

James II had two Protestant daughters – Mary the eldest, and Anne. This meant that there was no question of James being followed by a line of Catholic monarchs, and so people were not as worried by his attempts to encourage Catholics as they might have been.

In 1687 all this changed. The Queen gave birth to a boy. Boys came before girls in the line of succession. The boy was now heir to the throne – and he would be brought up as a Catholic.

William of Orange

Whigs and Tories united to invite William of Orange to come with an army to help them deal with James and make sure Mary, his wife, eventually inherited the throne. William had his own reasons for agreeing to this. His Protestant Dutch Republic was fighting a war against the Catholic King of France, **Louis XIV**. William needed England on his side. So he accepted the invitation.

activity

Work in pairs.
2 Look at the information in the text about Whigs and Tories on page 110. Why do you think:
a the Whigs decided to ask for William of Orange's help in 1688;
b the Tories also agreed with this?
3 Look at source 2 again. What is surprising about James II's behaviour when William landed?

James II runs away

No one is sure if William meant to make himself king. If James II had offered to call a Parliament and allow proper elections, most people would probably have stayed loyal to him. As it was, he panicked. He deserted his own army and escaped to France.

The English Parliament met and agreed that, because James had run away, he was no longer king. William refused to let Mary rule on her own, so Parliament invited them to become joint rulers as William III and Mary II. The Scottish Parliament did the same.

The Protestant succession

SOURCE 3

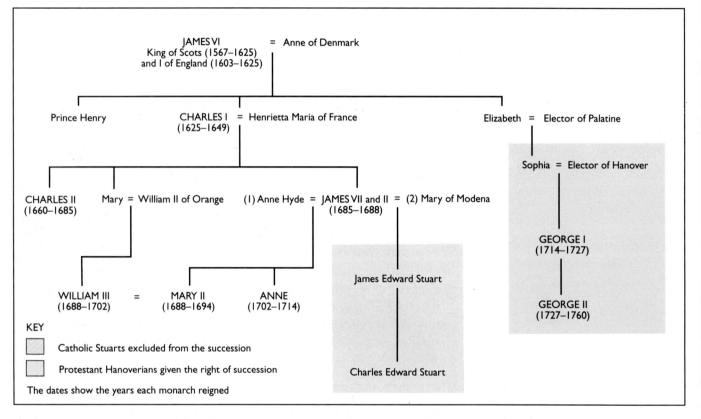

The Protestant Succession, arranged by the Act of Succession, 1701.

Parliament was determined that, in future, no monarch should be a Catholic. In 1689 it was agreed that if William and Mary (source 4a) had no children, they would be succeeded by Anne (source 4b) and that, then, Anne would be succeeded by one of her children.

But, in 1701, before Anne became queen, her ony surviving child, the Duke of Gloucester (source 4b), died. James II also died that year and Louis XIV of France recognised his son as James III and promised to help him to succeed to the throne.

Parliament, therefore, passed the Act of Settlement (source 3) to make sure that if either William (Mary died in 1694) or Anne died without children, the monarch would still be a Protestant. It said that the succession should pass first to the granddaughter of James I. This was Sophia, **Electress** of a small German state called Hanover. After that, it was to pass to her son, George (source 4c).

Sophia died in 1714, only a few months before Anne, who left no children. George, Elector of Hanover, then became King George I of the **United Kindom of Great Britain**, also of Ireland, and the founder of the Hanoverian line of monarchs (source 3).

> **i Electress** *Electress or Elector was the title given to those German princesses and princes who were allowed to take part in the election to choose the Holy Roman Emperor.*

> **i United Kingdom of Great Britain** *Great Britain became the official name of England, Wales and Scotland when James VI and I united the crowns of Scotland and England in 1603. In 1707, the kingdoms of England and Scotland became fully united (see Part 10) and officially known as the United Kingdom of Great Britain.*

SOURCE 4

JAMES VII and II	WILLIAM III and MARY II (until 1694)				
		ANNE	GEORGE I	GEORGE II	GEORGE III
1688	1702	1714	1727		1760

Kings and queens of Great Britain and Ireland, 1688–1760.

activity

1 What do sources 4a–4d and the information in the text suggest about how important Parliament thought it was to exclude Catholics from the throne?

SOURCE 4a

William III and Mary II. Mary died childless in 1694. William did not marry again and so died childless too. This painted plate was made during their reign.

SOURCE 4b

Anne, painted before she became queen, with her son, the Duke of Gloucester, who died in 1707.

SOURCE 4c

George I. He became king when he was fifty-four. He did not really want to leave Hanover and never bothered to learn English.

SOURCE 4d

George II. He became king at the age of forty-four and ruled for thirty-three years. He was a keen supporter of music and the arts, and was the last British king to lead his own troops into battle – at Dettingen in 1743.

activity

Work in pairs.
la What do you think would
(i) please, (ii) displease:
- Charles I
- John Pym
about the Bill of Rights?
Part 6, pages 67–70, will
help you.
b Discuss your ideas with
the rest of the class.
2 How does source 5
support the idea that the
Crown was very wealthy in
Queen Anne's time?

Changes in government

Crown and Parliament

In 1689, Parliament presented a Bill of Rights to William III and Mary II. This appointed them joint monarchs and settled once and for all many of the points that had been disputed between Crown and Parliament since before the Civil War. The Bill said:

1 Parliament alone could raise taxes, pass laws and control the army. The Crown could no longer do any of these on its own.
2 The Crown could not override laws.
3 Parliaments should be held frequently and members had the right to speak freely on all matters.
4 The monarch could not be a Catholic, or married to one, and had to take an oath to support and protect the Church of England.

In 1694 an Act was passed to say that a new Parliament should be called and elected every three years. In 1716 this was changed to every seven years.

The Crown continued to be responsible for the day-to-day government of the country. It still appointed ministers and dealt with foreign governments. But the Tory idea of Divine Right was dead. William and Mary were appointed to rule by Parliament, which had the power to alter the succession if it chose. The Crown was responsible to the people, not to God.

Money

After 1688, England fought two very expensive wars against France (source 5). Parliament supported these wars because it

SOURCE 5

Blenheim Palace, Woodstock, Oxfordshire. Queen Anne ordered the palace to be built for the Duke of Marlborough as a reward for his victory over the French at Blenheim, 1704. The architect was Sir John Vanbrugh, who said that, although the building was to be a private house, it ought also to be a 'royal and national monument'.

wanted to prevent Louis XIV from restoring James II and his son to the throne. The wars led to a big change in the way Parliament and taxpayers thought about money.

The Civil List

Parliament decided to give the monarch a guaranteed amount of money for life, to pay for the Royal Household and the staff of government. This money was called the Civil List. At the same time, Parliament took on the responsibility of paying for the armed forces, both in peacetime and in war.

Taxation

The quarrels between the earlier Stuart kings and Parliament had happened partly because Parliament would never give the Crown enough money. At last, landowners realised that they had to pay more taxes if they were to have a secure government and strong armed forces.

The Cabinet Council and the Prime Minister

The Cabinet

William III began the practice of choosing his chief ministers from those members of the Lords and Commons who had support in Parliament for their ideas. This meant that there would generally be support within Parliament for the government's policies.

After the Restoration, the large Privy Council became less important. Both Charles II and William III often used a Cabinet Council, which was a small group of Privy Councillors called together to advise the monarch about a particulary important matter. Under the Hanoverian kings, this smaller Cabinet Council became the chief council of government and it often met without the King.

The Prime Minister

In the early eighteenth century, people began to use the title 'Prime Minister' to describe the minister who appeared to be most powerful in the government and in Parliament. **Sir Robert Walpole** (source 6), First Lord of the Treasury under both George I and George II, is often called the first Prime Minister. But there was no official job called 'Prime Minister' and it was often unclear if there was one particular leading minister in the government at all.

SOURCE 6

Robert Walpole addresses the Cabinet Council.

Religious changes

The Quaker meeting house at Jordans, Buckinghamshire, built in 1688 when James II announced freedom of worship for Dissenters. After the Toleration Act of 1689, Quaker numbers grew.

In Scotland, as part of the agreement with William and Mary, the Presbyterian Kirk became Scotland's official Church and bishops were abolished.

In England, Parliament passed the Toleration Act in 1689. The Act allowed Dissenters, but not Catholics, to worship freely (source 7), but they still could not hold government office. After 1727 they were allowed to hold local government office.

In 1700 there were about 300,000 Dissenters. In 1800 there were 400,000. Before 1700 most Dissenters were landowning gentlemen; by 1750 the great majority were craftspeople and tradespeople.

activity

I How does source 7 show the confidence of some Dissenters in James II's promises?
2 What do you think would **a** please, **b** displease Oliver Cromwell about the religious changes made by the Toleration Act? Part 7, pages 89–92, will help you.

assignments

Ia William and Mary were invited to become king and queen in 1688 What were (i) the causes, and (ii) the consequences of this? Use the sources and information in Part 9 to help you to write a few lines about each cause and each consequence.
b Now divide both the causes and the consequences into
(i) immediate, (ii) short-term, (iii) long-term.
c Which (i) cause, (ii) consequence do you think was the most important? Explain your reasons.

2a Look back at the work you did for Assignment 4 in Part 7 or do the assignment now.
b Now use the sources and information in Part 9 to make charts or displays to show:
  (i) the powers of the Crown in 1700;
 (ii) the powers of Parliament in 1700;
(iii) religious arrangements in 1700.
c Do you think the events of 1688 led to more or less long-term change than the Civil War? Explain you reasons.
d Do you think (i) Whigs, (ii) Catholics, (iii) Dissenters, (iv) Tories would have described the changes brought about by the events of 1688 as progress? Explain your answers.

The United Kingdom and Ireland

In 1707 England and Scotland stopped being two separate kingdoms under one Crown and became one kingdom, united under one Crown, with one Parliament at Westminster. England, Wales and Scotland were then known officially as the 'United Kingdom of Great Britain'. Why did this union, which James VI and I wanted in 1603 and failed to achieve, happen in 1707, and what were the results?

James VI and I: King of Great Britain

When James VI of Scotland also became James I of England, following Elizabeth I's death in 1603, he united the two crowns – but not the two kingdoms. Scotland kept its own Parliament, its own laws and its own Church. James wanted to unite the two kingdoms completely and he was very disappointed when he found both his Scottish subjects and the English Parliament were against the idea. He told the Commons that those who opposed union preferred:

SOURCE 1

War to peace, trouble to quietness, hatred to love, and division to union.

James VI and I, *Speech to the House of Commons*, 1604

The truth was that the Scots and English were old enemies and the memory of this lived on. The Scots still remembered the claims of English kings in the Middle Ages to be their overlords. They recalled with pride their victory over the English at **Bannockburn** in 1314, but, in more recent times, there was also the memory of bitter defeats, especially at Flodden (source 2) in 1513.

In Elizabeth I's time, relations improved because the Scottish Church became Protestant and so the Scots and English needed each others' help against Catholic countries. But the English still thought of Scots as foreigners, living in a poor and uncivilised land.

> **i Bannockburn** In 1296 Edward I of England deposed the king of the Scots. In 1309 the Scots declared Robert Bruce to be their king. He led several successful campaigns against the English and, in 1314, defeated their army at Bannockburn.

SOURCE 2

The standard carried by the Earl Marischal (Marshal) of Scotland at the battle of Flodden, 1513. The French asked their ally, James IV of Scotland, to help them in a war against Henry VIII of England. The English army was better armed. The Scots were defeated and James IV himself, nine earls, fourteen lords and thousands of Scottish soldiers were killed.

activity

Work in pairs.
la Look at source 3 and the information in the text. What words do you think the English might have used to describe (i) the Scots (for example 'poor'), (ii) themselves.
b Look at the sources and information in Part 4, pages 44–47. Now list the words which you think the Scots might have used to describe (i) the English, (ii) themselves.
c Which words on each list do you think were most accurate?
d Discuss your ideas with another pair.

> **i** **Sir Anthony Weldon** had a job in James VI and I's Court. He visited Scotland with the king in 1617 and afterwards wrote his inappropriately named Perfect Description for which he was dismissed from his job. After that he wrote his hostile description of James in The Court and Character of James I (see source 22, Part 4).

Sir Anthony Weldon's comments were particularly biased and unpleasant:

SOURCE 3

The air might be wholesome but for the stinking people that inhabit it.

Sir Anthony Weldon, *A Perfect Description of the People and Country of Scotland*, 1617

Such views probably reflected the hostile attitudes of many English people. Above all, the English did not want Scottish merchants to be able to share in their wealth and trade.

James had to abandon his plan for a union, but he proclaimed himself 'King of Great Britain', much to the annoyance of the English Parliament, and had designs made for a new 'British' flag (source 4).

SOURCE 4

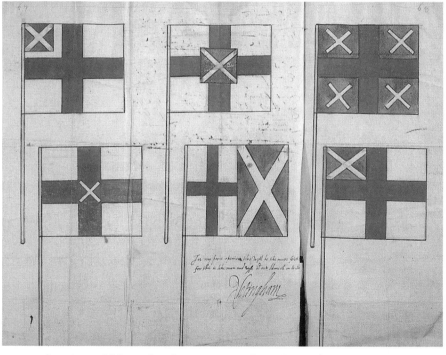

Designs for a 'British' flag. The idea was to combine the English flag, the red and white cross of St George, with the Scottish flag, the blue and white cross of St Andrew. You can see the flag that was actually used, flying on the front of the Great Charles (source 5, Part 6).

activity

2 Look at source 4. Imagine James VI and I puts you both on a committee to decide which design to choose for the new flag. One of you represents Scotland and the other England. What would you say **a** for, **b** against each design? Discuss your views.

Why did Scotland and England unite in 1707?

Neither Scots nor English were sorry when James VI and I gave up his plans for union. Yet, about a hundred years later, the idea was revived. What changed the minds of both sides?

The answer is that early in the eighteenth century, the Scots and the English found they needed important things from each other. The only way to get what they wanted was to negotiate a Treaty of Union.

The English need – the Protestant Succession

To make sure that the Catholic Stuarts did not return to the throne, the English Parliament passed the Act of Settlement in 1701 (source 3, Part 9). It arranged for Sophia of Hanover and her descendants to succeed to the throne if William III or Anne died without children. This Act had no force in Scotland, which was a separate kingdom.

It was vital for the English that the Scots should also agree to the Hanoverian succession. The Highlanders, in particular, were traditional Stuart supporters. The English were afraid that the Stuarts might return to Britain by what they called 'the back door'.

The Scottish need – wealth and trade

Scottish poverty: English wealth

Towards the end of the seventeenth century, England appeared to get richer and Scotland to get poorer. There were some bad harvests in Scotland and people died of famine, whereas English farmers produced a surplus of food after about 1650 (see page 126, Part 11) and there were no famines.

Meanwhile, English merchants were making huge profits from trade with English colonies in America (see page 127, Part 11) English laws said that only English merchants could trade with English colonies. Foreigners were banned; and after the end of the Republic in 1660, Scots were treated as foreigners as far as trade was concerned.

Scottish weakness: English strength

In 1695 the Scots set up a trading company of their own. They organised the **Darien Scheme** to found a Scottish colony in modern Panama. English merchants complained to William III that the competition would ruin their trade. William used his influence to stop English people putting money into the company and to stop English colonies from helping the Scots in Panama. In 1699 the scheme collapsed and the Scots blamed the English.

It was obvious that the English were powerful enough to prevent the Scots from trading on their own. Much as they disliked the English, many Scots decided that somehow they had to persuade them to allow Scottish merchants to share their trade.

The fear of war

The Scots realised that the English need for them to agree to the Hanoverian succession gave them the perfect chance to bargain. In 1704, the Scottish Parliament passed an Act of Security. It said that it would choose Queen Anne's successor when she died, and would not choose the monarch of England unless Scots were given the right to trade on equal terms with the English.

Anne needed money to fight a war with France. The Scottish Parliament told her that if she did not agree to sign this Act, it would not grant her money to fight the war against Louis XIV. She signed.

The English Parliament thought this was a stab in the back. It retaliated with an Aliens Act. This said that all Scots would be treated as foreigners and no Scottish goods would be allowed into England until the Scots recognised the Hanoverians as heirs to the Scottish throne.

The Scots were furious. The two countries were on the brink of a war, but neither side wanted one. The English needed to concentrate on Louis XIV and the Scots knew the English army was stronger than their's. The Scots noticed that the Aliens Act included the words:

SOURCE 5

If a nearer and more compleat union be not made between the said Kingdoms.

Aliens Act, 1705

They said they would be prepared to discuss some form of union if the English withdrew the Aliens Act. This was done. Commissioners from both kingdoms met in London to negotiate a union.

i Darien Scheme Darien was the name given by the Spaniards to an area of land on the north side of Panama where they founded a colony in 1510. Panama is an 'isthmus', a narrow piece of land with water on either side which connects two bigger pieces of land – in this case, North and South America. Today the Panama Canal cuts across the isthmus to link the Pacific and Atlantic Oceans. In the Darien Scheme the Scots planned to link the two oceans by setting up colonies on each side of the isthmus. Goods could then easily be transported by pack-animals from one to the other.

activity

I Use the sources and information on pages 119–120 to decide whether each of these statements is true or false.
a Some Scots thought they would be better off if Scotland and England united.
b The English wanted a war with the Scots to make them agree to the Hanoverian succession.

The Union

The Treaty of Union

SOURCE 6

The Commissioners present the Treaty of Union to Queen Anne, 1707.

> **i Federal**   A federal union is one in which two or more states join together to make one country with a central government, but each state continues to be in charge of running its own internal affairs. The central government usually looks after matters such as foreign affairs, defence and trade which concern the people of all the states. A country governed like this is called a federation. Federations today include the United States of America, Canada, Australia and Switzerland.

The Scottish commissioners wanted Scotland and England to keep their own Parliaments to look after Scottish and English affairs, while a Parliament of Great Britain looked after British affairs, such as relationships with foreign countries. This is called a **federal** union. The English commissioners refused to discuss this. They were interested only in the full union of the two countries, with one Parliament. In the end, the Treaty of Union arranged for:

- The Scots to send sixteen lords to the House of Lords and forty-five members to the House of Commons (England sent over 500).
- The Scots to have equal trading rights with the English.
- The Scots to agree to the Hanoverian succession.
- The English to pay the Scots compensation for their losses in the Darien Scheme (though the money eventually came from Scottish taxes anyway).
- The English and the Scots to use the same coins, weights and measures.
- The Scots to keep their own legal system.
- The Kirk to remain the official Church of Scotland.
- The two countries to use a common flag (source 7).

SOURCE 7

Cross of St George   Cross of St Andrew

Union Jack

The Union Jack of 1707. What are the differences between this flag and the one used today?

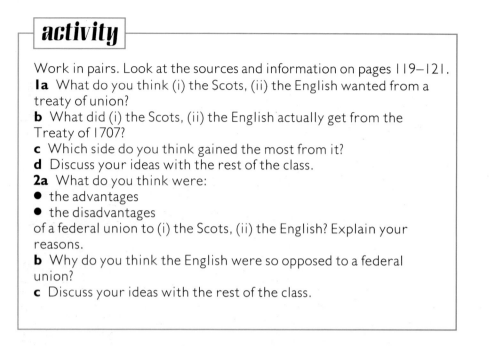

activity

Work in pairs. Look at the sources and information on pages 119–121.
1a What do you think (i) the Scots, (ii) the English wanted from a treaty of union?
b What did (i) the Scots, (ii) the English actually get from the Treaty of 1707?
c Which side do you think gained the most from it?
d Discuss your ideas with the rest of the class.
2a What do you think were:
● the advantages
● the disadvantages
of a federal union to (i) the Scots, (ii) the English? Explain your reasons.
b Why do you think the English were so opposed to a federal union?
c Discuss your ideas with the rest of the class.

The consequences of the Union

Its immediate unpopularity

The Union was very unpopular in Scotland, even though some people genuinely thought union was for the best. Its unpopularity increased after the Treaty. In particular, Scots did not like paying taxes to the government at Westminster, and they found that the English did not keep to their agreement and interfered in Scottish legal and Church matters.

The supporters of James VII and II's son, James Edward Stuart, were known as Jacobites because 'Jacobus' is the Latin word for James. In 1715 the Jacobites in Scotland took advantage of the unpopularity of both the Union and the new king, George I, to try to put James on the throne. The uprising was widely supported in both the Highlands and the Lowlands. But it was badly led by the Earl of Mar and it failed. Mar and James Edward escaped to France.

Scottish wealth and trade

By 1750, Scotland was far wealthier than it had been in 1700. The Union was not the only cause of this prosperity – but it helped. There was a large increase in the number of cattle Scottish farmers sent to London and sold there. Glasgow grew in wealth and size (13,000 inhabitants in 1708; 43,000 in 1780) because it became the main port for the import of tobacco from the colonies in America and for the export of linen, made nearby, in return. Scots also ran Britain's trade with Scandanavia.

The rebellion of 1745

SOURCE 8

The battle of Culloden, 1746. The artist is thought to have used Jacobite prisoners to model for him.

The increased prosperity of the Scots helps to explain the failure of the Jacobite rebellion of 1745, when James Edward's son, Charles Edward Stuart – 'Bonnie Prince Charlie' – landed in the Highlands. This time there was little support in the Lowlands and although Charles's army reached Derby in England, it found no support and retreated. The Highlanders were defeated at Culloden (source 8) by an army of English and Scots, which outnumbered them nearly two to one. The battle marked the end of Jacobite hopes.

The Highlands

The government used the Highlanders' support for the 1745 rebellion as an excuse to bring the Highland area fully under its control. Members of Highland clans were forbidden to carry weapons and to wear kilts or clan colours. The powers of clan chiefs to act as judges were ended. Many Highlanders, along with other Scots, went to start new lives in the colonies. Others joined Highland regiments within the British army.

activity

Work in pairs.

3 Look at source 8 and the information on pages 122–123.

a Which consequences do you think happened in (i) the short term, (ii) the long term?

b Which do you think were
- a gain
- a loss

for (i) the Scots, (ii) the English?

4 By 1750, most of the Scots and the English accepted the union of the two kingdoms.

a Suggest some reasons for this.

b Discuss your ideas with the rest of the class.

Ireland

In 1750, the monarch of the United Kingdom was also monarch of Ireland, but the two kingdoms remained separate until 1801. Dublin was the second largest city in the British Isles and an important centre for theatre and music. Irish merchants in London handled much of Britain's trade with France and Spain. Like the Scots, many Irish families were emigrating to the colonies and Irish men were serving in the British army. Yet, in Ireland itself most of the population had lost their rights as citizens and religious freedom.

The Jacobite defeat

When James VII and II left England in 1688, he went to France and then to Ireland where his many Catholic subjects still recognised him as king. From Ireland, he hoped to launch an invasion to restore himself to the thrones of Scotland and England. Louis XIV provided 7,000 French troops to help James, but his hopes ended in 1690 when William III crossed to Ireland and defeated him at the battle of the Boyne. The battle also ended Catholic Irish hopes of holding political power in Ireland.

Protestants and Catholics

SOURCE 9

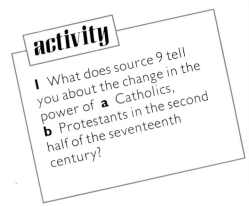

activity

I What does source 9 tell you about the change in the power of **a** Catholics, **b** Protestants in the second half of the seventeenth century?

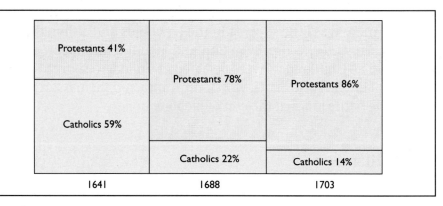

Protestants 41%	Protestants 78%	Protestants 86%
Catholics 59%	Catholics 22%	Catholics 14%
1641	1688	1703

Changes in the amount of land owned by Catholics and Protestants, 1641–1703.

Protestants had been steadily taking over the lands of Catholics since the mid-1600s. William's victory allowed the process of Protestant 'planting', or colonisation, to continue (source 9).

SOURCE 10

The Duke of Dorset's state ball at Dublin Castle, about 1751. All the important Protestant families in Ireland were there. In the eighteenth century, many wealthy Protestant families like these began to think of themselves as Irish rather than English.

Although they held most of the land in Ireland, Protestants were greatly outnumbered by the Catholic Irish. After 1690 the Protestants stopped Catholics from sitting in the Irish Parliament and passed laws to prevent them holding any form of office or military post. They also passed laws to take away the freedom of Catholics to worship, which William III had agreed to in the treaty ending the war in 1691.

activity

2 What does source 10 tell you about the power and wealth of some Protestant families in the early seventeenth century?

assignments

1 How might **a** Scottish Jacobites, **b** Scottish merchants disagree about the Treaty of Union? Why might the Jacobites have felt differently from many of the merchants?

2 Explain why Scotland and England united in 1707. What were the consequences of the union?

11

Luxuries and Manufactures

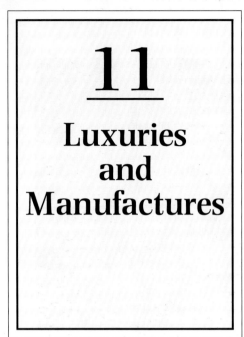

ℹ **Textiles** A textile is any cloth that is made by weaving. Linen, woollen, cotton and silk cloths are all textiles.

In the late seventeenth and early eighteenth centuries, many people in Britain, including some labourers, were wealthier. This was because, in around 1650, the increase in population (source 17, Part 5) slowed down. Farmers were producing masses of food, but there were fewer mouths to feed. As a result, the price of food stopped going up and, at last, labourers began to have some money to spare.

There were more things for people to buy and they could usually buy them near to home. More than 2,500 pedlars travelled around selling things at people's doors, and there were shops in many villages, as well as in the towns.

James Leach ran a shop in Bury, Lancashire. In 1668 he sold:

SOURCE 1

Textiles . . . *thimbles, pins, hooks and eyes, needles and threads . . . lace, tape and ribbon . . . knitted stockings for men, women and children . . . tea from India . . . sugar from the Americas . . . cheap tobacco . . . candles . . . spectacles . . .*

M. Spufford, *The Age of Expansion*, 1986

This tells us that, by the late seventeenth century, people living in one part of Britain could easily buy things made in another part. They could also buy luxuries from abroad.

SOURCE 2

A coffee house. The first coffee houses opened in Oxford in 1650 and in London in 1652. There were 80 in London by 1663. They were places to read newsheets and talk. They became popular as places for merchants to meet and do business.

Luxuries from abroad

Sugar, tea and coffee (source 2) were all popular luxuries for the better off in the late seventeenth century. Tobacco from the American colonies of Maryland and Virginia (source 3) was popular, too. It was an expensive luxury in 1620, when it cost £1–2 per lb. In 1700 so much was imported that it cost only 1 shilling per lb., and most people could afford it.

Many of these luxuries were available because of the growing trade with India and America. Because of the increase in this trade, many British merchants became very wealthy.

activity

1 What can you learn from sources 2 and 3 about some of the changes taking place in the late seventeenth century?

2 Look at the information about tobacco in the text.

a Do you think people in Britain thought of the use of tobacco as progress?

b What difference might it have made to their attitudes if they had known what we know today about the effects of smoking tobacco?

SOURCE 3

The dockside at Bristol. In the seventeenth and early eighteenth centuries Bristol grew to become the second largest English city after London. Its prosperity was the result of trade with the **American colonies** and the Caribbean Islands and Africa. Bristol merchants exported goods made in England to Africa. They exchanged these for slaves which they then took to the Caribbean and America to work on the plantations there. In return for slaves they were given sugar, tobacco and cotton which they took back to Bristol to sell at a profit.

> **American colonies** The first settlers to arrive in America from England were sent to Virginia by Sir Walter Raleigh in 1585, but they returned. The Virginia Company was founded later, in 1606. Puritan settlers sailing in the 'Mayflower' founded Massachusetts in 1620. Throughout the 17th century there was a steady increase in the number of settlers and of new colonies.

> **Manufactured** To manufacture originally meant to make by hand. Around 1600 it also came to mean to make something by physical labour, helped by machines.

British manufacturers

By the early eighteenth century, more things were being **manufactured** and sold in Britain than ever before. The rise in population in the sixteenth and early seventeenth centuries meant that more people, especially cottagers in the countryside, would take low wages in return for manufacturing work they could do at home. Merchants brought materials to their cottages and came back later to collect the finished articles. Textiles, lace, chains and nails were all made like this. This way of working continued after 1650 when the increase in population slowed down.

In 1726, the writer **Daniel Defoe** imagined a suit of clothes such as might be worn by 'the poorest countryman' or 'any servant in ordinary apparel'. He described how, in making up this suit, materials were used from 'almost all of the manufacturing counties of England' (source 4). This was a big change from 1600 when poorer people made clothes mainly from local materials.

> **i** **Daniel Defoe** (1660–1731) was a butcher's son who became a merchant dealing in stockings and socks. He was a Dissenter. Between 1703 and 1714 he was employed as a government spy to travel round the country and report on people's opinions. He wrote more than 550 books and pamphlets. The best known is the novel, Robinson Crusoe.

SOURCE 4

ITEM	MADE OF	MADE IN
Hat	Felt	Leicester
Coat	Cloth	Yorkshire
Shirt	Linen	Lancashire or Scotland
Buttons	Bone	Macclesfield
Buttons	Metal	Birmingham or Warwickshire
Gloves	Leather	Somerset
Waistcoat	Calimanco	Norwich
Lining	Shaloon (closely woven wool)	Berkshire
Breeches	Drugget (half wool, half linen)	Devizes
Stockings	Yarn	Westmorland

Where the materials for a labourer's suit of clothes came from. This is based on Daniel Defoe's description in his *Complete English Tradesman*, 1726.

Defoe said that the various items needed to make this suit could be bought:

SOURCE 5

> *In all the remotest towns and counties of England, be it where you will.*
>
> Daniel Defoe, *Complete English Tradesman*, 1726

This was possible because it was getting easier to transport things from one place to another. Between 1660 and 1750 about forty rivers were improved so that boats and barges could use them. Some roads were improved too, especially the main roads out of London. Carriers ran regular services to deliver packets and parcels by horse and cart between London and the other main towns.

activity

I What do sources 4 and 5 tell you about
a manufacturing,
b transport, **c** labourers in Britain in the early eighteenth century?